2002

# Crossing
# the
# Divide

*Dialogue among*
*Civilizations*

ISBN 0-9716061-0-2

# CROSSING THE DIVIDE

*Dialogue among Civilizations*

By

Dr. A. Kamal Aboulmagd, *Egypt*
Dr. Lourdes Arizpe, *Mexico*
Dr. Hanan Ashrawi, *Palestine*
Dr. Ruth Cardoso, *Brazil*
The Honorable Jacques Delors, *France*
Dr. Leslie Gelb, *United States of America*
Nadine Gordimer, *South Africa*
His Royal Highness Prince El Hassan bin Talal, *Jordan*
Professor Sergey Kapitza, *Russia*
Professor Hayao Kawai, *Japan*
Professor Tommy Koh, *Singapore*
Professor Hans Küng, *Switzerland*
Graça Machel, *Mozambique*
Professor Amartya Sen, *India*
Dr. Song Jian, *China*
Dick Spring, T.D., *Ireland*
Professor Tu Weiming, *China*
The Honorable Richard von Weizsäcker, *Germany*
Dr. Javad Zarif, *Iran*

Giandomenico Picco, *Italy*
Personal Representative of Secretary-General Kofi Annan
United Nations Year of Dialogue among Civilizations

With the support of:

School of Diplomacy and International Relations
Seton Hall University
Ambassador Clay Constantinou (Ret.), Dean
Marilyn DiGiacobbe, Associate Dean

and with
*Dr. Catherine Tinker, Project Director*

*To the innocents who lost their lives because
their only fault was to be
different from their murderers.*

# Table of Contents

# Foreword

The need for dialogue among civilizations is as old as civilization itself. But today, the need is more acute than ever. Individuals who live in fear and lack of comprehension of other cultures are more likely to resort to acts of hatred, violence and destruction against a perceived "enemy." Those who are exposed to the cultures of others and learn about them through communication across cultural divides are more likely to see diversity as a strength and celebrate it as a gift.

Today, globalization, migration, integration, communication and travel are bringing different races, cultures and ethnicities into ever closer contact with each other. More than ever before, people understand that they are being shaped by many cultures and influences, and that combining the familiar with the foreign can be a source of powerful knowledge and insight. People can and should take pride in their particular faith or heritage. But we can cherish what we are, without hating what we are not.

In shaping this endeavor, we are not starting from scratch. There is a set of common values that humanity has shared over centuries. The United Nations itself was founded in the belief that dialogue can triumph over discord, that diversity is a gift to be celebrated and that the world's peoples are united by their common humanity far more than they are divided by their separate identities. Indeed, the principles of the United Nations Charter and the Universal Declaration of Human Rights could be considered a common denominator for humankind.

I am thankful, therefore, that such a distinguished group of individuals has worked so effectively with my Personal Representative for the Dialogue among Civilizations in the preparation of this book. In a true spirit of dialogue, this work does not attempt to provide a manual of instruction, nor a prediction of the future. Rather, it offers reflections on diversity, a vision of our common humanity and a gateway to the dialogue, which is the responsibility of every one of us as human beings. I am sure many will benefit from it.

*Kofi A. Annan*
*October 2001*

# *Acknowledgments*

It was not easy to explain why the idea of a Dialogue among Civilizations was launched by the UN membership in 1998. Some would see its philosophical usefulness but not its practical relevance, while others even considered it a luxury when more immediate challenges had to be faced. However, by the end of the summer of 2001, I believe that very few would still retain those views. The events of September 2001, but not only, have made the pursuance of a dialogue across borders of all kinds quite necessary.

It is easy to say that this is an idea whose time has now come. Perhaps the brutality of those who do not believe in a dialogue among civilizations will encourage others, such as us, to take the issue more seriously.

In 1991, life gave me the chance to find myself blindfolded and taken away in the streets of Beirut to meet and negotiate with masked men who were holding hostages. One could say that the differences between us could not have been much greater. Yet we did communicate and we were successful. The so-called differences were no impediment to real communication. To me the seed for this book in a way was germinated then and there.

The manuscript could not have been done without the under-standing, support, advice, ideas and wisdom provided by the distinguished Group of Eminent Persons selected by the UN Secretary-General for this task. To all of them, I personally owe a debt of gratitude for their patience with me both during our drafting sessions and in our exchanges by e-mail and fax. They showed a great degree of tolerance for my, at times, undiplomatic way of making a point and my limited knowledge. They taught me what listening really means.

This project could not have been accomplished without the cooperation of a Secretariat that I had the pleasure of putting together thanks to Seton Hall University's School of Diplomacy and International Relations. It was Monsignor Robert Sheeran, President of the University, who opened the door for this cooperation between Seton Hall University and the United Nations. Ambassador Clay Constantinou, Dean of the School, and Marilyn DiGiacobbe, Associate Dean for External Affairs, carried a huge load, providing resources and helping to coordinate the project. I also wish to acknowledge the cooperation of the United Nations Association, and in particular Suzanne DiMaggio.

The very draft could hardly have seen the light of day without the care for detail, careful review and conceptual assistance of Dr. Catherine Tinker. She spent more time at the laptop in my office as we constructed the text than she bargained for. Teresa Hutsebaut provided more than just technical support, also encouragement and advice.

The faculty of Seton Hall's School of Diplomacy and International Relations were a needed sounding board for the manuscript, helping it take shape: Dr. Marian G. Glenn, Associate Dean; Dr. Margarita Balmaceda; Dr. Assefaw Bariagaber; Dr. Juan Cobarrubias; Ambassador S. Azmat Hassan; Dr. Robert Manley; Dr. Philip Moremen; Dr. Baron Piñeda; Dr. Courtney B. Smith; Dr. Jeffrey Togman; Dr. Gisela Webb; and Monsignor Robert Wister. They kept me on track when I was going off on a tangent. I wish to thank them all. I recognize it was not very easy to work with me.

I also wish to recognize the cooperation and support provided by research assistants Denise Del Priore and Bernard Waruta, and also Tonya Ugoretz for her assistance with the publication.

I wish to also extend my sincere appreciation to the governments of Austria, Ireland and Qatar and their Ministries of Foreign Affairs and Permanent Representatives to the United Nations in New York for their tremendous support of our meetings in Vienna, Dublin and Doha, which were quite remarkable.

I am most grateful to the Secretary General, H.E. Kofi Annan, for the opportunity he afforded me to be associated with a project I deeply believe in.

*Giandomenico Picco*
*October 2001*

# The Call for Dialogue

*I would like to propose, in the name of the Islamic Republic of Iran, that the United Nations, as a first step, designate the year 2001 as the "Year of Dialogue Among Civilizations," in the earnest hope that through such a dialogue the realization of universal justice and liberty may be initiated.*

*Among the worthiest achievements of this century is the acceptance of the necessity and significance of dialogue and the rejection of force, the promotion of understanding in the cultural, economic and political fields, and the strengthening of the foundations of liberty, justice and human rights. The establishment and enhancement of civility, whether at the national or international level, is contingent upon dialogue among societies and civilizations representing various views, inclinations and approaches. If humanity, at the threshold of the new century and millennium, devotes all its efforts to institutionalizing dialogue, replacing hostility and confrontation with discourse and understanding, it will leave an invaluable legacy for the benefit of future generations.*

*— Seyed Mohammad Khatami, President of the Islamic Republic of Iran, Speech to the United Nations General Assembly, UN Doc. A/53/PV.8, September 21, 1998*

# The Resolve of the United Nations

*The General Assembly . . .*

Welcoming *the collective endeavour of the international community to enhance understanding through constructive dialogue among civilizations on the threshold of the third millennium,*

1    Expresses its firm determination *to facilitate and promote dialogue among civilizations;*

2    Decides *to proclaim the year 2001 as the United Nations Year of Dialogue among Civilizations;*

3    Invites *Governments, the United Nations system, including the United Nations Educational, Scientific and Cultural Organization, and other relevant international and non-governmental organizations, to plan and implement appropriate cultural, educational and social programmes to promote the concept of dialogue among civilizations, including through organizing conferences and seminars and disseminating information and scholarly material on the subject and to inform the Secretary-General of their activities. . . .*

— *UN Doc. A/RES/53/22, November 16, 1998 (unanimously adopted)*

# INTRODUCTION

*Unity, Diversity and Hope*

# Unity, Diversity and Hope

**History has not ended** and **civilizations have not clashed,** even after September 11, 2001. Institutions, nations, groups and individuals are, however, being confronted with two contradictory trends: globalization and localization. While globalization in science and technology, mass communications, trade, finance, tourism, migration, crime and disease is progressing at an unprecedented pace and degree, the pervasiveness and depth of local identities defined in terms of ethnicity, language, land, religion and traditions have resurged as major forces in our time.

Market economy, democratic polity, civil society and individual rights as characteristics of modernization have assumed global significance; at the same time the strength of traditions in shaping the modern world has actually increased. The coexistence and mutual interaction between globalization and localization and the continuous presence of traditions in the modern world compel us to move beyond the simple mentality of "either-or."

World events of the last decade illustrated the inadequacy of some early 1990s theories. The dichotomy of "the West and the rest" that underlies the thesis of the "end of history" and "clash of civilizations" has proved to be too simplistic. At first read, the war between Azerbaijan and Armenia might be considered a good case in point; after all, one country is predominantly of one faith and the other of a different faith. Yet when the conflict developed, each side found its allies in the opposite "civilizational" camp, a situation that continues to prevail today years after the armed conflict has subsided. Kosovo, Bosnia and Vietnam offer similar poignant examples of finding allies across the divide.

The advent of the global village as virtual reality and imagined community is by no means solely an indication of integration and harmony. What the global village indicates is also difference, differentiation, demarcation, discrimination and dissonance. The world, compressed into an ecological, financial, trading and electronic system, has never been so divided in power, wealth, influence and access to information and goods. This seems to be the case at the international, regional, national and local level. In other words, the reality of real-time communication and borderless community has also brought to the surface the profound gap and even discrimination that coexists in the same territorial proximity. We can frequently be partners in conversation and professional life with associates thousands of miles apart, and yet be strangers to our neighbors. Real-time communication may be accessible to some and not to others, even within the same district.

The severity of the contrast between the "haves" and the "have-nots" at all levels of human experience—individual, family, society, nation and the world—feeds a pervasive mood of uncertainty. The pace and fluidity of change enhance the inability to cope, thus fueling bigotry, extremism, prejudice—in other words, all that reminds us of exclusion, the "either/or" mindset, the "us" and "them" mentality so familiar to us all.

We may have been misled into believing that the world has changed so much that the human condition is being restructured by newly emerging global forces without any reference to history and traditions. Yet one of our most significant reflections on globalization and the human condition is the acknowledgment that globalization does not necessarily mean homogenization, and that modernization intensifies as well as lessens economic, political, social, cultural and religious conflict in both inter- and intranational contexts.

The re-emergence of ethnicity, language, gender, land and religion as powerful forces in constructing our understanding of the world forces us to identify and develop new conceptual resources. The "end of history" may be the consequence of reading globalization as hegemonism and domination, and reading diversity as exclusion and threat. However, we may well be witnessing the beginning of a global history rather than the end. Our awareness of the danger of civilizational conflict rooted in primordial ties makes the necessity for dialogue particularly compelling. The politics of domination are being replaced by the politics of communication, networking, negotiation, interaction, interfacing and collaboration. The strong belief that modernization will wipe out cultural, institutional, structural and mental differences and, if unimpeded, will lead to a uniform modern world, is no longer tenable. Since globalization engenders localization as well as homogenization, cultural and institutional differences actually shape the contours of the modernizing process. In consequence, traditions are influencing the path of modernization, giving rise to distinctive cultural and institutional forms.

Resiliency and the explosive power of a deeply felt sense of belonging may inadvertently fuel the exclusivist passions to construct internally cohesive, but externally aggressive, cultural identities. The sense of self-worth is highly desirable unless it degenerates into self-centeredness. The sense of family cohesiveness is highly valuable unless it degenerates into nepotism. The sense of communal participation is useful unless it degenerates into parochialism. Patriotism is admirable unless it degenerates into chauvinistic nationalism. Human flourishing is essential unless it degenerates into a limiting anthropocentrism. If globalization is not to be hegemonism, it needs diversity; if localization is not to be exclusion, it needs common values.

**"Crossing the divide,"** whatever that divide seems to be, is the first step in the process of learning how to manage and appreciate diversity. It is a quality that new generations may find indispensable. Have we, the older generation, committed the sin of passing on the fear of diversity? We may well have. If that is so, it is equally important that the youth of our societies be aware of our mistake and find the courage to go a step farther, to learn what we have not, to see what we did not see and to extend a hand where we failed to do so. The young generation can and does aspire to do more and do a better job than we have done, to build a more just society than we have. No "lesson" from the past can dampen the dreams and aspirations, the visions and expectations, of the generation that is taking over. For most of us, the fact that something was not done before does not mean it cannot ever be done. This, if anything, is an incentive to strive for more.

If we have failed to cross the divide, to realize that diversity is not a synonym of "enemy," and in so doing we have built walls rather than tearing them down, it does not mean that the new generation cannot transform those walls into bridges and walk across them. A new generation can expect no less from itself than to do what previous generations have not done or have done poorly.

To those who may belittle and even ridicule us for trying to go beyond the world of "us" and "them," of governance through exclusion, of "enemy" as part of human nature, the young generation may wish to respond that such ridicule is simply the consequence of arrogance. This arrogance is to believe that what was achieved so far is the best that can be achieved. Well, we all know it is not. Is this not part of our human destiny: to explore, to discover, to strive, to reach, to achieve?

Yes, a dialogue is possible; will our generation be judged successful at it? If there will still be those who will accuse us of being idealists and dreamers, then let us admit that it is a sin of which many of us would like to be guilty. Sad is a nation whose young people have no dreams; sadder yet is a nation where the old try to kill the dreams of their young.

> *Few things have done more harm than the belief on the part of individuals or groups that he or she or they are in the <u>sole</u> possession of the truth: especially about how to live, what to be and do, and that those who differ from them are not merely mistaken but wicked or mad, and need restraining or suppressing. It is a terrible and dangerous arrogance to believe that you alone are right; have a magical eye which sees <u>the</u> truth and that others cannot be right if they disagree.*
>
> — *Isaiah Berlin,* Notes on Prejudice, *1981*

Diversity is a given, a law of nature shared by all species, human and nonhuman alike. People throughout history have always grouped themselves into clans, tribes and nations. This became clear when people started facing each other in greater numbers of contacts and recognizing their differences.

> *We have only one quarter the number of genes that scientists expected when the genome project started— only about twice as many as a fruit fly. . . . The difference between two human beings is minimal. Genetic determinism does not dictate how you and I turn out.*
>
> — *Craig Venter, President of Celera, quoted in* Financial Times, *Dec. 31, 2000*

The problem is not the fact of diversity itself, but rather the perception of diversity as a threat. The fact that different languages and written scripts emerged at about the same time in diverse forms—hieroglyphics, cuneiform, linear script, calligraphs—has not been perceived as a threat.

> *O mankind! We created*
> *You from a single (pair)*
> *Of a male and a female,*
> *And made you into*
> *Nations and Tribes, that*
> *Ye may know each other*
> *(Not that ye may despise*
> *Each Other).*
>
> — Qur'an, *Sura 49:13, Abdullah Yusuf Ali translation*

Our sense of belonging is not exclusive. We are part of our family, but also of our community, our linguistic group, our religious denomination, our professional brotherhood, our nation, our continent and finally, our human species. Yes, we do have multiple identities in the same individual.

# CHAPTER 1

*Overview*

# Overview

## A. The Context of Dialogue:
### *Why Dialogue and Why Now?*

Whatever our different visions and experiences of the past century, we seem to agree that exclusion was the rule in the first half and even the first three-quarters of the century; and that inclusion has made some headway, but not everywhere, during the last forty years. We seem, however, to have a different perception of what the twentieth century meant, in terms of change of paradigm, that is a set of different points of reference by which to read societal growth or evolution. Whether it was Wilsonian principles, the 1945 United Nations Charter or the Treaty of Rome establishing the European Union, it seemed that the realization of inclusion was hard to come by, and perhaps it is. As the twentieth century came to a close, we all felt that on the one hand we could see the incredible and positive changes of mindset among individuals and entire nations. But on the other hand, we witnessed a spiral of tragedies linked to the fear of diversity and, indeed, to the perception that diversity is a threat. In a way, it was like an ill wind of misconceptions sweeping away the possibility for dialogue, for inclusion and indeed destroying beyond recognition the common humanity that binds us all. Yes, the 1990s began on the wrong foot as far as the Dialogue is concerned, where fear of diversity took the ugly face of ethnic cleansing, religious confrontations and even "clash of civilizations." Yet there was also a great desire to find alternatives where the fear of diversity could be bridged by dialogue and a recognition of our common future.

As diversity swings in the balance, two opposing features seem to dominate today's society. On one hand, there is a trend toward homogenization the likes of which we have not seen before. On the other hand, we have also seen the blossoming of identities where we had groupings and commonalities, the rise of many different voices demanding to be heard and the claim to participation made by smaller and smaller units, even by groups as small as one individual.

The 1990s also taught us that achievements in social management can be reversible. We have had integration and disintegration; globalization and localization; communication across the planet and the rebirth of new isolationisms: ideological, religious or political. We have seen the emergence of a sole superpower. We have seen the big affecting the small, but we have also seen the small affecting the big, as the financial crises of the last decade have shown. It is perhaps this two-way street that has become the true sign of the new times. No longer will only the most powerful make its mark on human endeavors. Not only will the most powerful state call the shots, so to speak, but also even smaller states, and indeed groups and individuals, will be able to be heard.

The 1990s have brought home that the number of players on the international scene has dramatically increased. They are no longer only the nation states: nongovernmental organizations (NGOs), institutions, corporations and even single individuals will shape the future of international society. Despite the concern for global homogenization and the overwhelming power of the strongest, decision-making across the globe is more fragmented than ever. The strong and the weak are both contributing to the shaping of what is yet to come more than at any other time in human history. Yes, the great concern is the hegemonism of the strongest, but an equally true reality is the ability of so many to have their voices heard, for better or for worse, and to contribute to change, whatever it might be. But "voices being heard" does not mean "roles being given." The need is to be aware of the changes underway, and to have the courage to accept changes that are effected at speeds unimaginable only a few decades ago.

Perhaps the most relevant feature of the last part of the twentieth century was and is the speed and pace of change. If we look at the state of the world as a computer model, where the basic hardware—the institutions that are the machinery of civilization—have been recognized world-wide, we would also have to say that the software—namely, the rules and codes of conduct, the rules of management and the actors present—do not seem to fit the hardware itself. We may therefore be observing a fundamental mismatch between hardware and software, needs and capabilities. Participation in the entire system is no longer the sole province of traditional power centers. For better or worse, the stage has become more crowded.

The speed of change is forcing us all to learn faster. Learning faster may mean widening our horizons and exchanging experiences with as many diverse groups and individuals as possible. The learning process may well be directly linked to the variety of experiences. It may also be directly linked to the acceptance of diversity as a source of wider learning. Periods of isolationism have been synonymous with poverty in some countries, a mistake never again to be repeated by those who have experienced it.

The 1990s were marked by indignities suffered by those caught in conflicts incited and justified by individuals—be they leaders or followers—on the basis of ethnic, religious, tribal, cultural, gender or other perceived differences. Those who committed these indignities presented them first as the consequences of social, political, economic and other diversities; then they attributed them to a collectivity; and third, they told us they were unavoidable. Unfortunately, very few voices were raised to challenge these fallacies of the presumed dimensions of the conflicts. One would have walked in vain through the killing fields of Cambodia, or the Balkans, or the African great lakes region seeking the "killing hand of history," "the raping arm of culture," the "destructive boot of any institution," or the "mutilating fist of religion." The search would have been useless, for the only entity on this earth able to commit those indignities was, is and will be the individual human being, whether leaders or members of groups; no one and nothing else.

By the mid-1990s, one wondered how many individuals on this planet still had faith in the indomitable spirit of human beings, in their ability to discover what is yet to be known, and in their determination to overcome the most difficult problems, to search to the end of the earth for a better life and to fight injustice no matter how hard. So many seemed to accept the inevitability of what happened. Had the human spirit been captured by the fallacy of a predetermined destiny that accepted as unavoidable the maiming of children and the destruction of thousands of victims?

Ideologies based on perceiving diversity as a synonym of enmity and indeed as a threat seemed to flourish in the 1990s, as if the need for an enemy were a necessity of life. How far had we gone wrong as a human species to lose even the courage to raise our voices and cry foul? By September 2001, the overwhelming majority of the world finally cried out loud that no religion, no history, no ideology and no traditions could justify or call for the perversity of terrorist acts. The responsibility of those individuals could not be hidden under these false pretenses. Where innocents lost their lives because their only fault was to be different from their murderers, the large majority of humanity realized that no justification could be invented. Yes, the perpetrators of the September 11 attacks would love to see a clash of civilizations. They could not exist without an enemy. Were the events of September 11 instead an indication of a clash within one civilization, a struggle, in other words, for the soul of what they claim to be their civilization?

*What we do not have, however, is a war between Islam and Christianity, because the overwhelming majority of Muslims around the world have condemned the attacks.*

— *Tommy Koh,* International Herald Tribune, *September 26, 2001*

Why, then, a Dialogue among Civilizations? Within this context, the answer seems to be quite simple. Is there not a need for a new global ethic? Is there not a need for a new appreciation of diversity, particularly now that we know that differences are so paper-thin? After all, are we not only "six degrees of separation" apart from one another, at most? Why is it that so many see the differences, and so few appreciate the commonality? Or is it perhaps that those who fear the differences are determined to make them even deeper, and those who recognize the reality of commonality rest silent, relying on the strength of that truth? Perhaps the real answers to all these questions can only be found if we accept that divisions and separations by groups, no matter how defined, will never be a true representation of reality. Not only in each group at any given time will we find people who coexist with different mindsets, but beyond that we may have to accept that each of us individually harbors at different times, at different moments, even if to a different degree and only occasionally, both the perception that diversity is a threat and the perception that commonality unites us all. The Dialogue, in other words, starts first within ourselves.

## B. The Goal of Dialogue:
*Towards a New Paradigm of Global Relations*

Dialogue is a proper instrument to achieve a new paradigm of global relations. Dialogue is the first step in providing a sense of belonging, for by communicating and listening we take the first step toward recognizing our own commonality.

Our Dialogue presupposes the existence of common, universal values. For too long, a misconception has prevailed that rationality, liberty and tolerance, as well as justice and respect for human dignity, belong to the West; this assumption has been challenged in more than one way. To be sure, some of these values clearly originated in Asia and in Africa much before they came to be appreciated in Europe. We recognize the existence of a "global common denominator," which some may call a "global civilization," meaning to us common ethical standards and values, the foundation for a global ethic.

By engaging in dialogue, we—from various regions of the globe—are honoring an ancient practice, seeking respectful communication and mutual understanding, but always grounded in the practical reality of living at this time in a diverse universe. Dialogue begins from a common starting point, identifying common principles such as equity and the "Golden Rule." Dialogue as a process then can be used to address specific areas or problems in politics, society, economics, environment, education and ethics. To be useful, a dialogue is open, based on knowledge and a search to know and appreciate differences. It is a true conversation about common values, universal norms and particular practices, seeking convergences as well as allowing divergences.

> *We appeal as human beings to human beings to remember your humanity and forget the rest. If you can do so, the way lies open to a new paradise.*
>
> — *Bertrand Russell and Albert Einstein, signatories,* Manifesto, *July 9, 1955*

It is probably true that in the collective imagination, the danger of a nuclear catastrophe of planetary dimension has been removed. Whether it is in reality removed or not is another matter. And it is equally true that the risk of proliferation of weapons of mass destruction has not yet caught the imagination of many. What seems to be true is that ignorance has been used to feed the fear of diversity in so many societies and across so many divides.

Indeed the overwhelming paradigm of international relations in past centuries has been one where the nation-state was the monopolistic actor on the international scene and diversity was silently—or not so silently—accepted as the discriminant element to describe the enemy.

Another element of that old paradigm of international relations is that having built a system for collective decisions, we have also fed the belief in collective responsibility rather than individual responsibility. We have learned over the last several decades to attribute responsibility to institutions, as well as to even less well-defined concepts like history, religion and civilizations. The international system has done its best to shield the individual from direct responsibility in matters that pertain to the state *(res pub-lica)*.

It is true that over the last few decades we have begun to move out of this worldview in a modest, gentle fashion. Some sixty years ago, the community of nations at large refused to accept the excuses of those who claimed that they were not individually responsible for their deeds because they were simply "obeying orders." Today perhaps we should be equally firm and refuse to accept those who try to hide their individual responsibility behind the concepts of ethnicity, gender, religion, history and even civilizations.

Can we move to a worldview of inclusion, of participation, of humanizing the differences and of accepting the many commonalities that unite us? The key to a new paradigm of global relations is to overcome the misunderstanding that diversity is a synonym of enmity. How might this look?

> *On July 20, 2000, on the shores of Lake Tiberias, two young families were enjoying a summer day, strangers to each other. A young boy decided to swim in the waters of a lake that touches three countries. A few minutes into his joyful swim, he was overwhelmed by panic or fatigue, and he gasped for air. From the shore, the first to notice was a young man, father of the other young family. Instinctively, he dove into the waters and within minutes he rescued the young boy, who managed with a bit of help to regain the shore and the safety of the sands. Unfortunately, the young man who saved the boy was physically overcome and drowned. What history recorded of that day on Lake Tiberias is*

*that the young boy who was saved was of the Jewish faith and the young father who helped him was of the Muslim faith. Under the new paradigm, one father had saved the life of a young boy who was not his own, as any parent would do, no matter when, no matter where, even at the cost of his own life.*

— *Based on widespread news reports, July 2000*

The goal of the Dialogue among Civilizations may seem impossible to achieve for some. What we suggest as dialogue is to look at each other with different eyes; that is, not with the eyes of the past, but with the eyes of the future, a future where we will unavoidably be closer together in more ways than one. It is the conceptual focus of what will make the management and utilization of diversity more practical to achieve.

The new paradigm will have to make clear that is not a synonym for enmity, and that globalization is not the opposite of individual identities. We seek a fuller meaning of inclusion, of participation, of contributions, of voices, than ever before, a worldview in which diversity is seen as a source of strength, and of wealth, and as a tool of betterment.

It is perhaps fitting here to remember that immediately after the Cold War, we witnessed a rush of intellectual and political theories to invent or to discover a new enemy. Those theories may have had limited success, but the old paradigms have not disappeared; the mindset that perceives diversity as a threat is still alive and kicking. To be successful, the paradigm shift will have to happen in the minds of individuals.

Science seems to indicate that human beings are more similar than dissimilar. If indeed genetic determinism does not dictate the attitudes of individuals, then the very concept of xenophobia may have no biological basis. At the level of society, the new paradigm will be able to undermine the necessity for the enemy as a managerial tool in society, and challenge the too-convenient concept of collective responsibility. Though collective decisions may be a fact, responsibility basically remains individual; for otherwise, the commitment of each of us to the collective decision will be very weak indeed. Individual commitment to the collective decision will also challenge the perception that might inevitably makes right.

Our Dialogue among Civilizations is a dialogue *within* societies as well as *between* and *among* them. This dialogue leads us to recognize what unites us across any divide: a commonality as we seek a better life for all our children. This is a commonality that unites us when we feel that there are components of our daily life that cannot be surrendered under any circumstance: our humanity, our ability to forgive, our sense of justice, a larger purpose that we alone can never define or achieve. Can we call that perhaps the sense of belonging to one human family, one where each group, individual or nation will be welcomed for the positive contribution it offers and will not be feared as a threat projected onto others?

## C. A Different Way of Looking at the United Nations

Our Dialogue among Civilizations seeks to find a new way of looking at our neighbors, globally, locally and even individually, and also to understand the significance of the United Nations. That enterprise is universal in dimension and yet focused on respect for each individual identity. It is an endeavor that is deeply rooted in the history of this and earlier centuries, as so many elements of the United Nations still reflect the past: the overwhelming relevance of the major powers and the sacrosanctity of the nation-state. Yet it is also an enterprise that contains seeds of a future vision, specifically indicated by the acceptance of two concepts: governments and peoples. Our aspiration is to a system where a voice is heard not because it is richer or has a higher pitch than others, but simply because it is part of the universe of nations and peoples. As a human endeavor, it is based on what the world has been and is, but it also claims to sketch what the world *could* be. It contains the realism of what has happened and the aspiration towards what is yet to be.

Much of the work of this new worldview is contained in the very philosophy of the United Nations. Perhaps it is also true that much of the philosophy and vision of the United Nations has been blurred, set aside and at times disregarded by the prevailing old paradigm, one of bigotry and prejudice, of exclusion and of a mindset that sees diversity as a threat. In the 1990s, one could have easily wondered why, when some of the major walls of division and separation had just come down, so many rushed to erect new ones. For those who needed ignorance to feed the fear of diversity, the walls had to be tall indeed. It is no surprise, therefore, that the United Nations found it almost impossible to handle those conflicts generated not by ideological competition, not by differing priorities, not even by different economic visions of the future or for that matter social construction, but by the simple mindset that diversity itself is a threat. Those indignities and those conflicts were and are the very nemesis of the United Nations, the very opposite of the values of the United Nations Charter and the ultimate challenge to the future of the United Nations because they negate the very core of the world organization.

The challenge that these indignities of the 1990s presented for the international system at large was existential, not functional. Yet it seems that many looked at the United Nations' unsuccessful endeavors in those years as a problem of functionality—a technical matter, so to speak; an issue of structures, perhaps a question of appearances. Rather, the indignities of the 1990s questioned the very principle of human dignity, the very interpretation of diversity, the very aspiration of universality and the very achievements of the international community since 1945. One could argue that those so-called ethnic conflicts or acts of human intolerance were perpetrated by individuals who, by their actions, had put themselves outside the framework of the United Nations. Otherwise, why would they have attacked the very fundamentals on which the founders based the human enterprise called the United Nations?

The vision and the philosophical foundation of the United Nations that we would like to rediscover is the one based on what we may call the "global social contract." We are, of course, aware that the main reason for the establishment of the world body was to prevent another world war. If universality is an inherent feature of the organization, it follows that its members are individually recognized. Their individuality and their belonging to the same common family is another inherent characteristic of the organization. Therefore, there exists a common denominator among all of them. The undeclared global social contract is among the members of the organization: on one hand, those who seek to be included and to participate in the collective decision-making process, and on the other hand, those who seek, from the other members, legitimacy for their policies.

Looking at the United Nations in this way, of course, does not mean looking at its structures and the mechanics of the organization, but rather at the United Nations as a place where a contract can be consummated that would provide the best recognition of each other's identities and the acceptance of the common belonging. The new paradigm of global relations based on inclusion that we are trying to sketch will therefore make the work of the United Nations more successful and its machinery more efficient, as much as the old paradigm of enmity and exclusion have made it at times paralyzed and, at best, occasionally successful. The meaning of our intellectual journey goes beyond restructuring of the United Nations.

Eventually seeing the United Nations as the place where a global social contract is consummated—one that includes "participation" in the decision-making process and provides "legitimacy" to those who propose ideas and solutions—will lead us to consider also the role of the new actors on the international scene who can hardly be excluded from a Dialogue among Civilizations. They are the organizations of civil society, the individuals, indeed maybe also the economic units, that move the world economy. From education to mobilization to providing basic relief services, NGOs have demonstrated their willingness to act when states are unable, or just unwilling, to do so.

As the pace of globalization accelerates, private enterprises are increasingly seen as key players for better or for worse in the process of building societies for all of the world's peoples. Large corporations have operating expenses and profits that far exceed the budgets of many of the world's countries. A major portion of global trade is actually cross-border flows of capital and goods within individual firms. As a result, some businesses are active players in our efforts to promote economic development, transfer appropriate technology and training, protect the global environment and fight against transnational social ills like crime and disease. Others may be encouraged to contribute to these efforts, although not all will share these goals; some may, in fact, be on the other side in their single-minded quest for profits. In any case, private enterprises are major players whose actions inevitably affect the lives of many people.

Finally, individuals operating outside the sphere of traditional government-to-government diplomacy have clearly demonstrated their ability to influence events around the globe. From religious leaders to former political leaders, from social activists to writers and artists and, lamentably, from terrorists to drug dealers to money launderers, people now have the ability, for good or bad, to dramatically affect the lives of their fellow human beings. As a result, the challenge of learning to appreciate diversity lies with each and every person.

*Harmony without uniformity.*

— *Confucius*

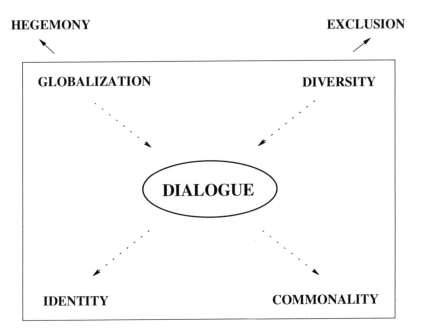

Figure 1

# CHAPTER 2

*The Context of Dialogue:*
*Globalization and Diversity*

# The Context of Dialogue: Globalization and Diversity

As we move beyond the dichotomies of globalization and localization, developed and developing, capitalism and socialism, we become an increasingly interconnected global village. By transcending the assumed dichotomies of tradition and modernity, East and West, North and South and us and them, we can tap the rich and varied spiritual resources of our global community as we strive to understand the dilemmas of the human condition. At a minimum, we realize that the great religious traditions that had significantly contributed to the "Age of Reason"—the Enlightenment of the modern West—contain profound meaning for shaping the lives of people throughout the world. Christianity, Judaism, Islam and Greek philosophy are and will remain major founts of wisdom for centuries to come. Other ways of life, notably Hinduism, Jainism, Buddhism, Confucianism and Daoism, are also equally vibrant in the contemporary world and will most likely continue to flourish in the future. Moreover, scholars as well as policy makers have recognized that indigenous forms of spirituality—such as African, Shinto, Maori, Polynesian, Native American, Inuit, Mesoamerican, Andean and Hawaiian—are also sources of inspiration for the global village.

Western, non-Western and indigenous traditions are all immensely complex, each rich in fruitful ambiguity. Actually, the monotheistic religions (Judaism, Christianity and Islam) all originated from the East and symbolize an age-long process of substantial transformations. Similarly, the Hindu, Buddhist, Confucian and Daoist ways of life are each the unfolding of a spectacular spiritual vision involving fundamental insights, elaborate rituals, social institutions and daily practice. Our awareness of the richness and variety of the spiritual resources available to the global community enables us to rise above our hegemonic and exclusive arrogance and seek the advice, guidance and wisdom of other traditions. Furthermore, we also fully acknowledge the danger of inter- and intrareligious conflicts that seriously threaten the stability of local, national and regional communities, creating major challenges to cultivating hope worldwide. The need for a dialogue is obvious.

## A. Globalization and the Human Condition

Accompanying the rapid globalization of the last decade was an increasingly heated debate over its merits and demerits. Globalization has produced new bodies of knowledge, falsified "self-evident" conventional truths and created myths and misperceptions of its own. Forces of globalization include the explosion in information and communications technologies, rapid expansion of the market economy, dramatic demographic change, relentless urbanization throughout the world and the trend toward more open societies. In the economic sphere, private capital in direct investments and portfolio funds has grown rapidly, the reduction of tariff barriers has become a pervasive worldwide phenomenon, the demand for transparency of financial institutions is increasing, and concerns about corruption are spreading.

These by-products of economic globalization have exerted great pressure on governments to become more publicly accountable, thus creating new possibilities for democratization. As a result, civil societies, symbolized by the formation of transnational NGOs, have emerged as important actors in national, regional and international politics. Surely, the idea that "the rising tide carries all boats" seems to be working. While the rich are getting richer, the poor are not necessarily becoming poorer. Some countries that have opened their economies, reduced tariff barriers and encouraged two-way foreign trade seem to have benefited from the new global situation. However, we recognize that open borders for goods do not yet apply sufficiently to agricultural products, a development that would be welcome, of course, and benefit the countries of the South. Already, in the last thirty years, some industrialized states and some developing countries have made strides in eradicating abject poverty in the direction of development and peace. It seems that we are moving from an old world of division and walls to a brave new world of connections and webs.

Yet, with 20 percent of the world's population earning 75 percent of the income and 25 percent earning less than 2 percent, 31 percent illiterate, 80 percent living in substandard housing, more than a billion people living on less than a dollar a day and nearly a billion and a half people without access to clean water, the state of the world is far from encouraging. Furthermore, the widening gap between the haves and have-nots and the rampant commercialization and commodification of social life, including the life of family, school and religious institution, undermine the civic solidarity of developing countries and threaten the moral fabric of societies in developed countries. Anxiety over the loss of cultural identity and the weakening of communal ties is widespread, and retreat to ethnic and other parochial loyalties has become an easy way of dealing with such anxieties. Can globalization lead us to a more promising land or will it generate more conflicts and contradictions in our already tension-ridden world? Is there a better way to manage globalization so that its blessings are spread more uniformly?

## From Westernization and Modernization to Globalization

> *Globalization is an intensification of the process of human interaction involving travel, trade, migration, and dissemination of knowledge that have shaped the progress of the world over millennia.*
>
> — *Amartya Sen,* The New York Review of Books, *July 2000*

Present-day globalization may well have to be seen in a larger historical perspective. The spread of Buddhism from Benares, Christianity from Jerusalem and Islam from Mecca are historic cases in point. Globalization was also seen in commercial, diplomatic and military empire-building. Indeed, the intercivilizational communication among missionaries, merchants, soldiers and diplomats in premodern times was instrumental in fostering proto-globalization long before the advent of the industrial and information revolutions. The fifteenth-century maritime exploration significantly contributed to bringing the world together into a single "system." Similarly, colonialism and imperialism have brought once disparate peoples into close contact with each other. Western Europe has substantially reshaped human geography and left an indelible imprint on the global community.

Modernization theory, formulated in the 1950s in the United States, asserts that the "modernizing" process that began in the modern West was actually "global" in its transformative potential. The shift from the spatial idea of Westernization to the temporal concept of modernization is significant, suggesting that developments that first occurred in Western Europe, such as industrialization, cannot be conceived simply as "Western" because they were on their way to becoming Japanese, Russian, Chinese, Turkish, Indian, Kenyan, Brazilian and Iranian as well. This was precisely why the nongeographic idea of temporal modernization seemed to better capture the salient features of Westernization as a process of global transformation.

However, implicit in modernization theory was the assumption that development inevitably moves in the same direction as progress and, in the long run, the world will converge into one single civilization. Since the developed countries, notably the United States, were leading the way, modernization was seen as essentially Westernization and particularly Americanization. This narrative is, on the surface, very persuasive because the characteristics of modernity and the achievements of modernization, as defined by the theorists, are not merely Western or American inventions. Market economy, democratic polity, civil society and individual rights are arguably universal aspirations.

Events in recent decades clearly show that the competitive market has been a major engine for economic growth. They also show that democratization is widespread, that a vibrant civil society encourages active participation in the political process and that respect for the dignity of the individual is a necessary condition for social solidarity. These developments may have prompted several scholars to argue that there is no longer any major ideological divide in the world: Capitalism has triumphed, market economy and democratic polity are the waves of the future and "history" as we know it has not ended.

Nevertheless, the euphoric expectation that the modernizing experience of one civilization would become the model for the rest of the world was short-lived. Samuel Huntington's warning of the coming clash of civilizations was perhaps intended to show that as long as conflicting worldviews and value systems exist, no nation, no matter how powerful and wealthy, can impose her particular way upon others. In the twenty-first century, the most serious threats to international security will not be economic or political but cultural. At first blush, the "clash of civilizations" theory seems more persuasive than the "end of history" advocated by Francis Fukuyama, because it acknowledges that culture is important and that religious difference must be properly managed. Unfortunately, its underlying thesis is still "the West and the rest," and it recommends a course of action that presumes that the West will eventually prevail over its adversaries.

Warnings about imminent civilizational conflict make a dialogue among civilizations not merely desirable, but necessary. Even the most positive definition of modernization—market economy, democratic polity, civil society and individual rights and responsibilities—allows room for debate and discussion about its feasibility. The free market evokes questions of governance; democracy can assume different practical forms; styles of civil society vary from culture to culture; and whether dignity must be predicated on the doctrine of individual rights has no easy answer. Modernization is neither Westernization nor Americanization. The fallacy of "the West and the rest," like that of "us and them," is its inability and unwillingness to transcend the "either-or" mentality. Globalization compels us to think otherwise.

Westernization and modernization are clearly antecedents of globalization, but between them is a quantum leap in terms of the rate of change and the depth of conceptual transformation. Information technology, the prime mover of economic development, has had far-reaching political, social and cultural implications. Although the promise that the "knowledge economy" can help poor countries leapfrog over seemingly intractable stages of development has yet to become a reality, information exchange at all levels has substantially increased throughout the world. Similarly, although geography still matters greatly in economic interchange and income distribution, new information and communications technologies have the potential to significantly change international income inequalities. An axiom of our age is that the lines of wealth, power and influence can be redrawn on the world map in such a way that the rules of the game themselves must be constantly revised. Especially noteworthy is the great emancipatory and destructive potential of emergent globalizing technologies. Robotic machines and computers can sequence the human genome, design drugs, manufacture new materials, alter genetic structures of animals and plants and even clone humans, thus empowering small groups of individuals to make profound positive and negative impacts on the larger society.

Conceptually, globalization is not a process of homogenization. For now, at least, the idea of convergence—meaning that the rest of the world will eventually follow a single model of development—is too simplistic to account for the complexity of globalizing trends. Surely, environmental degradation, disease, drug abuse and crime are as thoroughly internationalized as science, technology, trade, finance, tourism and migration. The world has never been so interconnected and interdependent. Yet, the emerging global village, far from being integrated, let alone formed according to a monolithic pattern, is characterized by diversity and, recently, by a movement towards assertiveness of one's identity. The contemporary world is, therefore, an arena where the forces of globalization and its opposite—localization—are exerting tremendous pressure on individuals and groups.

## Local Awareness, Primordial Ties and Identity

One important reason for this diversity and increased assertiveness of one's identity is that globalization accentuates local awareness, consciousness, sensitivity, sentiment and passion. The resurfacing of strong attachments to "primordial ties" may not have been caused by globalizing trends, but it is likely to be one of their unintended consequences.

We cannot afford to ignore race, gender, language, land, class, age and faith in describing the current human condition. Racial discrimination threatens the solidarity of all multiethnic societies. If it is not properly handled, even powerful nations can become disunited. Gender equality has universal appeal. No society is immune to powerful women's movements for fairness between the sexes. Linguistic conflicts have ripped apart otherwise stable communities in developed as well as in developing countries. The struggle for sovereignty is a pervasive phenomenon throughout the world. The membership of the United Nations would be expanded several times if all separate identities were to seek international recognition. The so-called North-South problem exists at all levels—international, regional, national and local. The disparity between urban and rural is widening in developing countries; urban poverty presents a major challenge to all developed countries. Generation gaps have become more frequent—the conventional way of defining a generation in terms of a thirty-year period is no longer adequate—and the struggle between generations more intense. Fissures among siblings are often caused by lifestyles influenced by different "generations" of music, movies, games and computers. Religious conflicts occur not only between two different faiths but also between divergent traditions of the same faith. Not infrequently, intrareligious disputes are more violent than interreligious ones.

In short, the seemingly intractable conditions, the "primordial ties," that make us concrete living human beings, far from being eroded by globalization, have become particularly pronounced in recent decades.

> *Globalization may erode the authority of the state, and alter the meaning of sovereignty and nationality, but it increases the importance of identity. The more global our world becomes, the more vital the search for identification.*
>
> — *Elmer Johnson, President, Aspen Institute*

Indeed, it is impractical to assume that we must abandon our primordial ties in order to become global citizens. Further, it is ill advised to consider them necessarily detrimental to the cosmopolitan spirit. We know that our strong feelings, lofty aspirations and recurring dreams are often attached to a particular group, expressed through a mother tongue, associated with a specific place and targeted to people of the same age and faith. We also notice that gender and class feature prominently in our self-definition. We are deeply rooted in our primordial ties, and they give meaning to our daily existence. They cannot be arbitrarily whisked away more than one could consciously choose to be a totally different person.

Since the fear that globalization as a hegemonic force will destroy the soul of an individual, group or nation is deeply experienced and vividly demonstrated by an increasing number of people—for example, riots in Seattle against the World Trade Organization in December 1999 and protests in Davos against the World Economic Forum in January 2000—we need to take seriously the presence of primordial ties in the globalizing process. Only by working with them, not merely as passive constraints but also as empowering resources, will we benefit from a fruitful interaction between active participation in global trends that are firmly anchored in local connectedness.

Realistically, primordial ties are neither frozen entities nor static structures. Surely, we are born with racial and gender characteristics, and we cannot choose our age cohort, place of birth, first language, country's stage of economic development or faith community. Ethnicity and gender roles, however, are acquired through learning. Moreover, our awareness and consciousness of ethnic pride and the need for gender equality is the result of education. Our sensitivity, sentiment and the passion aroused by racial discrimination and gender inequality, no matter how strong and natural to us personally, are the results of socialization and require deliberate cultivation. This is also true with age, land, language, class and faith. They are all, under different circumstances and to varying degrees, culturally constructed social realities. In this sense, each primordial tie symbolizes a fluid and dynamic process. Like a flowing stream, it can be channeled to different directions.

While primordial ties give vibrant colors and a rich texture to the emerging global community, they also present serious challenges to the fragile world order and to human security. The United Nations, which arose from the cosmopolitan spirit of internationalism, is compelled to deal with issues of identity charged with explosive communal feelings. The pervasiveness of racial prejudice, gender bias, age discrimination, religious intolerance, cultural exclusivity, xenophobia, hate crimes and violence throughout the world makes it imperative that we understand in depth how globalization can enhance the feeling of personal identity without losing the sense of integrally belonging to the human family. Primordial ties are, of course, not a static notion.

We recognize that the concept of change is inherent in every culture and civilization, and that to a large extent, the fear of change is intertwined with the notion of enemy. We also recognize that civilizations have adapted to changes, so much so that they now share views on many issues.

> Globalization has brought countries and civilizations increasingly closer to one another. More similarities and a host of fundamental common values are discovered in the course of convergence of civilizations. . . . The development of globalization will create broader space for the development of civilizations, each with its own unique characteristics.
>
> — Song Jian

Perhaps one of the most salient dimensions of globalization is economic globalization. It is often measured by aggregate growth, productivity rates and returns on capital investment. Other indicators, such as eradication of poverty, employment, health, life expectancy, education, social security, human rights and access to information and communication are essential to improve the quality of life. The idea of the stakeholder, rather than shareholder, can enable an ever-expanding network of people to participate in this potentially all-inclusive process. We may not be the beneficiaries of market economy, but we all have a stake in maintaining the quality of life of this earth.

Undeniably, global economic institutions can enhance the quality of life; they were established to favor financial stability and eventually to foster balanced economic growth. Obviously, there are apparent winners and losers in a competitive market, and the pervasiveness of the cultural and linguistic influence of a particular region in a given moment may be unavoidable. But, if globalization is perceived as the domination of the powerful either by design or by default, it will not be conducive to international stability. Since globalization is not homogenization, imagined or real hegemonism is detrimental to the cultivation of a culture of world peace. The Dialogue among Civilizations is intended to reverse this unintended negative consequence of globalization.

### Dialogue as Mutual Learning

Ordinary human experience tells us that genuine dialogue is an art that requires careful nurturing. Unless we are intellectually, psychologically, mentally and spiritually well prepared, we are not in a position to engage ourselves fully in a dialogue. Actually, we can relish the joy of real communication only with true friends and like-minded souls.

How is it possible for strangers to leap across the so-called civilizational divide to take part in genuine dialogue, especially if the "partner" is perceived as the radical other, the adversary, the enemy? It seems simpleminded to believe that it is not only possible, but realizable. Surely, it could take years or generations to completely realize the benefits of dialogical relationships at the personal, local, national and intercivilizational levels. At this time, we propose only minimum conditions as a turning point on the global scene.

Our urgency is dictated by our concerns for and anxieties about the sustainability of the environment and the life prospects of future generations. We strongly believe in the need for a new guardianship with a global common interest. We hope that, through dialogue among civilizations, we can encourage the positive forces of globalization that enhance material, moral, aesthetic and spiritual well-being, and take special care of those underprivileged, disadvantaged, marginalized and silenced by current trends of economic development. We also hope that, through dialogue among civilizations, we can foster the wholesome quests for personal knowledge, group solidarity, self-understanding and individual and communal identities.

We have learned from a variety of interreligious dialogues that tolerating difference is a prerequisite for any meaningful communication. Yet, merely being tolerant is too passive to transcend the narrow vision of the "frog in the well." We need to be acutely aware of the presence of the other before we can actually begin communicating. Awareness of the presence of the other as a potential partner in conversation compels us to accept our coexistence as an undeniable fact. This leads to the recognition that the other's role (belief, attitude and behavior) is relevant and significant to us. In other words, there is an intersection where the two of us are likely to meet to resolve divisive tension or to explore a joint venture. As the two sides have built enough trust to see each other face-to-face with reciprocal respect, the meeting becomes possible. Only then can a productive dialogue begin. Through dialogue, we can appreciate the value of learning from the other in the spirit of mutual reference. We may even celebrate the difference between us as the reason for expanding both of our horizons.

Dialogue, so conceived, is a tactic of neither persuasion nor conversion. It is to develop mutual understanding through sharing values and creating a new meaning of life together. As we approach civilizational dialogues, we need to suspend our desires to sell our ideas, to persuade others to accept our beliefs, to seek their approval of our opinions, to evaluate our course of action in order to gain agreement on what we cherish as true and to justify our deeply held convictions. Instead, our purpose is to learn what we do not know, to listen to different voices, to open ourselves up to multiple perspectives, to reflect on our own assumptions, to share insights, to discover areas of tacit agreement and to explore best practices for human flourishing. Only then can we establish mutually beneficial relationships based on reciprocity.

## B. Diversity and Community

We need to remind ourselves, time and again, that neither the historical contingencies and the changing circumstances, nor the differences in color, ethnicity, language, educational background, cultural heritage and religious affiliation among us, mitigate against our common humanity. Our genetic codes clearly indicate that, by and large, we are made of the same stuff. The idea that we humans form one body not only with our fellow human beings but also with other animals, plants, trees and stones—"Heaven and earth and the myriad things"—expresses a cosmic vision as well a poetic sense of interconnectedness. We may even be able to trace all our ancestries to one source, if not to the African mother as proposed by some scholars. The African proverb that the earth is not only bequeathed to us by our ancestors but also entrusted to us by generations to come elegantly illustrates the undeniable fact that we have lived and will continue to live on this planet together.

While we affirm our common humanity, we are wary of faceless or abstract universalism. We are acutely aware that diversity is necessary for human flourishing. Just as biodiversity is essential for the survival of our planet, cultural and linguistic diversity is a defining characteristic of the human community as we know it. However, socially derived and culturally constructed perceptions of differences are used for setting individual against individual, group against group and majorities against minorities. The resultant discrimination yields to strife, violence and systematic violation of basic rights. While we celebrate diversity, we condemn ethnocentric and other exclusivist forms of chauvinism.

The space between faceless universalism and ethnocentric chauvinism is wide and open. This is the arena in which intercivilizational dialogues can take place. Great ethical and religious traditions have shaped the spiritual landscape of our world for millennia. Communication across ethnic, linguistic, religious and cultural divides has been a salient feature of human history. Despite tension and conflict between and among the divides, the general trend toward more contact and interaction across these divides has never diminished. Historically, each great ethical and religious tradition has encountered different belief systems and faith communities. Indeed, their vitality has often resulted from these encounters. By learning from others, the horizon of a given tradition became significantly broadened. For example, Christian theology benefited from Greek philosophy, Islamic thought was inspired by Persian literature and Chinese intellectual history was enriched by Indian ideas with the arrival of Buddhism in the first century.

Nevertheless, the fear of the other has also led to strife and prolonged struggle. So-called interreligious wars are common throughout history. The peaceful interaction of two major civilizations, such as the Indian transformation of the Sinic cultural universe and the introduction, assimilation and incorporation of Mahayana Buddhist schools into the Chinese spiritual landscape, is rare. Since harmony among religions is essential for cultivating a culture of hope for the human family, interreligious dialogues are an integral part of the Dialogue among Civilizations. The opportunity for all religions, including emerging ones, to affirm unity of purpose for the promotion of the common public good is unprecedented in human history. More recently, globalization has substantially increased the density of interreligious communication.

The idea of the "common public good" is predicated on the advent of a global community. A global village, as an imagined virtual reality, is not a community. The term "community" ideally implies that people live together, share an ethos and a practicable civic ethic and are unified in their commitment to the common good. Such a unity of purpose, however, allows for diversity in lifestyles and differences in belief, so long as the diversity and differences do not infringe upon the fundamental freedoms and rights of others. Although we are far from realizing a true sense of community in the global village, we hope that global and local trends congenial to this development continue to accelerate, and that traditional and modern practices appropriate to it continue to spread.

As we reflect upon the past and meditate on the future we would want for our children, the question that looms large in our minds is: How can we embrace diversity by living responsibly—respectful of others' traditions and yet faithful to our own—in the emerging global community? Real acceptance of diversity compels us to move beyond genuine tolerance to mutual respect and, eventually, to celebratory affirmation of one another. Ignorance and arrogance are the major roots of stereotyping, prejudice, hatred and violence in religious, cultural, racial and ethnic contexts. While physical security, economic sustenance and political stability provide the context for social integration, real community life emerges only if we are willing to walk across the divides and act responsibly and respectfully towards one another. Through dialogue, we learn to appreciate others in their full distinctiveness and to understand that diversity, as a marvelous mixture of peoples and cultures, can enrich our self-knowledge. Dialogue enhances our effort to work toward an authentic community for all.

> *African traditional religion is increasingly recognized for its contribution to the world. No longer seen as despised superstition which had to be superseded by superior forms of belief, today its enrichment of humanity's spiritual heritage is acknowledged. The spirit of Ubuntu—that profound African sense that we are human only through the humanity of other human beings—is not a parochial phenomenon, but has added globally to our common search for a better world.*
>
> — *Nelson Mandela*

The Dialogue among Civilizations presupposes the plurality of human civilizations. It recognizes equality and distinction. Without equality, there would be no common ground for communicating; without distinction, there would be no need to communicate. While equality establishes the basis for intercivilizational dialogues, distinction makes such joint ventures desirable, necessary, worthwhile and meaningful. As bridge-builders committed to dialogue, we recognize that there are common values in our diverse traditions that bind us together as women, men and children of the human family. Our collaborative effort to explore the interconnectedness of these values enables us to see that diversity empowers the formation of an open and vibrant community. Our own experience in multicultural encounters, our shared resolve to break down divisive boundaries and our commitment to address perennial social concerns have helped us to identify the values critical to the promulgation of responsible community.

## C. Common Values

As never before in history, the emerging world community beckons us to seek a new understanding of the global situation. In the midst of a magnificent diversity of cultures, we are one human family with a common destiny. As our world becomes increasingly interdependent, we identify ourselves with the whole global community as well as with our local communities. We are both stakeholders of our own respective countries and of one world in which the local, national, regional and global are intricately linked. A shared vision of common values can provide and sustain an ethical foundation for a dialogue among civilizations. We recognize that the complexity of contemporary life may generate tensions between important values. The task of harmonizing diversity with unity is daunting; the conflict between private interests and the public good may seem unresolvable; and the choice between short-term gains and long-term benefits is often difficult. Yet, we believe that a new sense of global interdependence is essential for our ongoing collaborative effort to foster a worldwide mindset of hope.

> *From the Ten Commandments to Buddhist, Jain, Confucian, Hindu, and many other texts, violence and deceit are most consistently rejected, as are the kinds of harm they make possible, such as torture and theft. Together these injunctions, against violence, deceit, and betrayal, are familiar in every society and every legal system. They have been voiced in works as different as the Egyptian Book of the Dead, the Icelandic Edda, and the Bhagavad-Gita.*
>
> — *Sissela Bok,* Common Values, *1995*

We affirm, from the outset, that we are for the protection of individual freedoms, for guarantees of fundamental rights and for the recognition of and respect for the equal worth of every human being. These are the Enlightenment values of the modern West and underlie a market economy, a democratic polity and civil society. While none of them is fully realized in any given society, they are universal aspirations. Indeed, liberty, rights and personal dignity have universal appeal, but so also do duty, human responsibility and the good of the community. They provide us with a fuller agenda to begin our reflection. The cultivation of a sense of duty and the protection of individual freedoms can work together to allow the human spirit to soar without the danger of social disintegration. The encouragement of human responsibility and the guarantee of fundamental rights can complement each other to give people a secured space for thought and action without threatening the fabric of social cohesiveness. The requirement that each act responsibly to one another (the community) and the recognition of and respect for the equal worth of every human being offer a balanced approach to the relationship between self and society.

> *Without the individual impulse, community stagnates; without the sympathy of the community, individual impulse fades away.*
>
> — *William James*

The mutually beneficial interplay between self and society assumes a new shade of meaning in our time. We need to examine it in personal, local, national, regional and global contexts. We also recognize that transcendence of the divisiveness of self-interest requires moving beyond national and regional as well as personal and local concerns. Global forces beyond our comprehension easily overwhelm us and "ethnic and religious conflicts" beyond our control easily immobilize us, as if we cannot escape the predicament of the two extreme forms of destruction: domination and disintegration. Nevertheless, we hope that, with the advent of a dialogical global community, we can, for the first time, talk about the human family in the realistic sense of communication and interconnection. We want to stress that globalization has frightening aspects. It may bring about hegemonism and monopolism, for example, but this is not inevitable. Similarly, despite bigotry and exclusivism in identity politics, the authentic quest for identity is a noble calling and an educational experience for our children and us.

> Our eyes grow heavy with weeping,
> yet a brook can make us smile.
> A skylark's song bursting heavenward
> makes us forget it is hard to die.
>
> There is nothing now that can pierce my flesh.
> With love, all turmoil ceased.
> The gaze of my mother still brings me peace.
> I feel that God is putting me to sleep.
>
> —Gabriela Mistral, "Serene Words"

We choose to reject faceless universalism, hegemonic control and monopolistic behavior on the one hand and ethnocentric bigotry, religious exclusivism and cultural chauvinism on the other. We believe that positive forces in globalization and authentic quests for identity can create a virtuous circle uplifting the human spirit in the coming decades. Wholesome globalization, which celebrates diversity and enhances community, is a matter of confluence, of mutual learning and recognition of the rich and varied human heritage. This allows for lateral and reciprocal relationships among civilizations and makes genuine dialogue possible. In such a dialogical mode, the echoes of each civilization awaken, encourage and inspire the others. The resultant sympathetic resonance is a truly cosmopolitan harmony, cross-cultural and trans-temporal.

To this end, we wish to note that the most fundamental and pervasive value underlying all common values is humanity.

To understand the profoundly rich meaning of humanity, we begin with an exploration of the Golden Rule. Whether stated in the positive ("do unto others what you would want others to do unto you") or the negative ("do not do unto others what you would not want others to do unto you"), the Golden Rule is shared by virtually all the great ethical and religious traditions. It was identified by the Parliament of World Religions in 1993 as the basic principle in the emerging global ethic. We believe that the awareness, recognition, acceptance and celebration of the other in our own self-understanding, implicit in the Golden Rule, help us to learn to be humane.

### Humanity, Reciprocity and Trust

Learning to be humane (or, straightforwardly, "human") is a defining characteristic of all classical education, East or West. It is a profoundly meaningful challenge in the contemporary world as we move beyond perhaps the most brutish century in human history. The idea of humanity, perceived inclusively and holistically, is applicable to every person under all circumstances. While we transcend race, language, gender, land, class, age and faith in asserting our conviction that the dignity of the human person is inviolable, we need to learn to treat each individual person humanely, whether a poor old white man, a Chinese merchant, a Jewish rabbi, a Muslim mullah, a rich young black woman or anyone else. This requires an ability to see difference not as a threat but as an opportunity to broaden humanity.

Our learned capacity to reject stereotyping, prejudice, hatred and violence in religious, cultural, racial and ethnic contexts is predicated on the value of reciprocity. Reciprocity is an integral component of the Golden Rule, a guiding principle present in all of our spiritual traditions. Strictly speaking, however, the Golden Rule stated in the negative—"do not do unto others what you would not want others to do unto you" — is required for true reciprocity. This seemingly passive attitude considers the integrity of the other without imposing our will, even if we honestly believe that our way is the best for everybody. This self-restraint is predicated on the belief that what is best for me may not be appropriate for my neighbor. In matters of taste or preference, this is easily understandable, but, in the context of religious pluralism, even faith cannot be exempted from the principle of reciprocity. Indeed, the spirit of dialogue can be dampened if the intention to proselytize overwhelms the necessity to listen and to learn first.

Nevertheless, the Golden Rule stated in the positive need not be in conflict with the spirit of reciprocity at all. While "do unto others what you would like others to do unto you" does not give us the license to impose our faith prematurely on anyone else, it instructs us to be concerned about others and actively involved in their well-being. Reciprocal respect, necessary for genuine dialogue, enables us to engage others in true partnership. Only when our conversational partners feel understood and appreciated can we take an active role in involving them in a mutually beneficial joint venture. Thus, the Golden Rule stated in the negative allows for creative engagement and the Golden Rule stated in the positive prevents the passivity of indifference toward the suffering of the other. Whether stated in the negative or in the positive, the Golden Rule cultivates interpersonal trust.

Trust enables dialogue to occur, to continue and eventually to bear fruits. It is the backbone of true communication. Without trust, we can do little to facilitate any meaningful communication. Trust is not blind. It is a rational choice to enter into communication with the other. It is the minimum condition for transcending the psychology of fear. Unless we can move out of our self-imposed cocoons and face up to the challenges of the unknown, we will never be able to rise above our egoism, nepotism, parochialism and ethnocentrism. Mistrust inhibits any cross-cultural collaborative effort and stunts the growth of a culture of peace. Trust is a commitment to the possibility of an ever-enlarging community. It is the source of mutual respect and understanding. Trust enables us to accept the other as an end rather than a means to an end.

Trust is not opposed to a healthy dose of skepticism or the critical spirit, but it is never hostile to the other or cynical about the actual state of affairs. Despite tensions and conflicts in the world, trust involves a willingness to explore commonality and shareability with those who are stereotyped as radical others. Trust is the courage to enter into a joint venture with a stranger who is conventionally labeled as the enemy. Through trust, we respect the integrity of the other as a matter of principle and also as an end in itself. While a trusting person may sometimes be disappointed and deceived, it does not deflect him or her from the commitment to continuous communication within and beyond family, society and nation. Trust involves keeping promises and seeing one's action through. Yet, it is dictated by a higher principle of rightness. If promise-keeping will be harmful to the overall well-being of a person (for example, lending money to a drug abuser), it is right to break the promise. Similarly, if an initiated action is likely to lead to disastrous consequences, such as the development of an environmentally unsound power plant, discontinuing the action is right.

To assume trust in the integrity of the other is to be fair-minded and respectful. It is the beginning of true dialogue. The need for trust in any business transaction or contractual agreement is obvious, but trust in interpersonal and cross-cultural communication is even more important. While legal actions can be taken to remedy commercial misconduct or a breach of contract, all possibility of communication simply evaporates between persons and cultures when trust is absent. A sense of fairness can generate a spirit of trust; with trust, it is easy to put justice into practice. Similarly, a humane person is trusting and trustworthy. Motivated by sympathy and compassion, a humane person establishes an ever-expanding network of interpersonal and cross-cultural relationships. Trust is implicit in these relationships. With trust, legal constraints are simply preventive measures. When interchange among peoples and cultures is conducted in good faith, civility pervades the process and mutual learning ensues. If we have faith in the Dialogue among Civilizations, we can learn not merely from the wisdom of our own tradition but also from the cumulative wisdom of the entire human community.

Humanity and trust engender the ethos of mutual flourishing in interpersonal relationships at both individual and communal levels. They are the preconditions for discussing common values. Without humanity and trust, there is no underlying common ground for exploring values as a joint spiritual venture of like-minded dialogical partners. In light of this discussion, we wish to identify the following sets of common values for focused investigation: liberty/justice, rationality/sympathy, legality/civility and rights/responsibility. Since the values of liberty, rationality, legality and rights have been more thoroughly elucidated in contemporary political discussions, we choose to emphasize the importance of justice, sympathy, civility and responsibility as equally significant values for the emergence of the global community. We believe, if fully recognized, these four common values can help to facilitate dialogue among civilizations; such dialogue can substantially enhance the possibility of realizing a global ethic.

## Toward a Global Ethic

### Liberty and Justice

If humanity helps us to relate meaningfully with our fellow human beings, justice is the practical method of putting this value into concrete action. A humane world is necessarily just. Gender inequality and racial discrimination are unjust. So are major discrepancies in income, wealth, privilege and accessibility to goods, information or education.

Since the widening of the gap between the haves and have-nots is an unintended negative consequence of globalization, we are particularly concerned about the marginalized, disadvantaged and silenced individuals and groups in the human family. They deserve our focused attention and our persistent support. We believe that the more influential and powerful an individual, a group, a nation or a region is, the more obligated he, she or it is to improve the well-being of the human community. It is not practicable or even just to impose an arbitrary principle of egalitarianism on individuals and groups, but it seems only right to ask that the beneficiaries of globalization share their resources more equitably with the world. Justice means that public policies tend toward benefiting the weaker. It is humane and just to figure out ways to empower the marginalized, underprivileged, disadvantaged and silenced.

Justice as fairness is a call to higher standards of behavior. The eradication of poverty is a prominent just cause in the emerging global community. How can we help to build capacities to enable the poor to rise out of their poverty? How can we educate women and girls so that they can break away from the vicious cycles of population pressure and economic underdevelopment? How can we encourage the leadership of the North and successful economies elsewhere to recognize that the elimination of poverty, regardless of where it occurs, is integral to their national interests? How can we appeal to the conscience of people worldwide to see that poverty anywhere is a global concern? Such questions need to be addressed at local, national, regional and global levels.

We think these questions are being slowly addressed. The commitment at the 1995 Social Summit in Copenhagen to "accelerate the development of Africa and the least developed countries" is predicated on a realistic model of interdependence. If we consider ethnic, cultural, linguistic and religious diversity as a global asset, Africa could not be solely characterized as the continent of the HIV epidemic, poverty, underemployment and social disintegration alone. It could also be recognized as a rich reservoir for human spirituality and the cumulative wisdom of the elders. The African spirit, symbolized by the geological and biological diversity of the tiny area around Cape Town, South Africa, said to be comparable in richness to the vast area of Canada, ought to be a source of inspiration for a changed mindset that addresses social development as a global joint venture. The fate of Africa is important for non-Africans as well because, without a holistic sense of human flourishing, we cannot properly anchor our security, let alone our well-being, in the global community as a whole. Indeed, Africa has provided such lessons.

> When the Prophet Muhammad sent his oppressed followers to the African Christian King Negus of Abyssinia for safety, and they received his protection, was that not an example of tolerance and cooperation to be emulated today? . . .
>
> The nature of interaction between the strands of our religious heritage could help lay solid foundations for the establishment of a world order based on mutual respect, partnership, and equity. On a continent battling against the scourge of underdevelopment, AIDS, ecological disaster, and poverty, competition

*amongst religions will be utterly misplaced. Tolerance and cooperation, on the other hand, will give the moral leadership so gravely needed.*

— *Nelson Mandela*

It is neither romanticism nor sentimentalism that compels us to focus our attention on Africa. While sympathy, empathy and compassion propel us to form solidarity with our brothers and sisters in agony, justice impels us to recognize that our well-being is at stake if even a corner of the world, let alone a continent, is in grave peril. A limited short-term rational calculation may fail to show any tangible linkage between Africa's problems and the self-interests of other regions, but common sense tells us that, since interdependence has become a fact of life in the global community, ignorance and neglect of a substantial part of the world is detrimental to human security in the long run. Indeed, the abusive treatment of any one of us diminishes the sacredness of humanity as a whole.

Dialogue among civilizations is inclusive. It is an open invitation to all members of the global community. Justice, founded on fairness, assures us that all willing participants are allowed in the dialogue without discrimination. Justice, based on fairness, further encourages wider participation by actively involving those on the periphery. Those who perceive dialogue as an exercise in futility or merely a dispensable luxury, because the burning issues of basic survival overwhelm them, could particularly benefit from positive engagement in an ongoing dialogue. In fact, their presence in a fair-minded interchange (sharing stories for example) can help to improve the behavior, attitudes and beliefs of those immune to the plight of the marginalized. At the same time, the causes of and solutions to urgent problems can be put in a new light. Often, injustice on the part of political leadership (the lack of transparency, public accountability and fair play) is the main reason for economic and social crises. The issues can be more clearly identified and more effectively managed from a comparative cultural perspective.

### Rationality and Sympathy

Human beings have often been defined as rational animals. The ability to know our self-interest, to maximize our profit in a free market or to calculate our comparative advantages indicates that we are capable of instrumental rationality. Rationality, or more appropriately reasonableness, is also essential for interpersonal relationships, acquisition of knowledge, political participation and social engagement. Humaneness, however, involves sympathy, empathy and compassion as well. Humanity as a value cannot be realized through rationality alone. The ability to treat a concrete person humanely is not the result of rational choice but of sensitivity, conviction, commitment and feeling.

Attachment to and intimacy with those who are close to us is one of the most natural and common human experiences. We cannot bear the suffering of those we love. This sense of commiseration is often confined to our children, spouse, parents, immediate kin and close friends. If we can extend this personal feeling to commiserate with those we like, to those we care for, to those we barely know and even to strangers and beyond, our sense of interconnectedness will be greatly enhanced. We may never truly experience the lofty ideal of forming one body with humanity, but if we aspire to the moral dictum that we should treat all human beings as brothers and sisters, we will try to establish harmonious relationships with an ever-extending network of interconnectedness. The need for dialogue among civilizations is based on care for the other.

It is often assumed that while rationality is objectively veri-fiable and publicly accountable, sympathy, as a matter of the heart, is personal and private. Surely, as an emotive state, sympathy cannot be easily described in precise lan-guage or rigorously defined in quantitative terms. Nor can it necessarily be demonstrated as a generalizable quality of the human psyche. We all hope that human beings learn to be sympathetic, but we cannot ensure the universality of sympathy across race, culture and religion. Under the influence of Greek philosophy, for example, we are willing to assert that human beings are rational animals, but we are reluctant to insist that sympathy is a defining charac-teristic of human nature as well.

However, in a comparative civilizational perspective, both Confucianism and Buddhism maintain that sympathy, em-pathy and compassion are at the same time the minimum requirement and the maximum realization of the human way. According to Confucian and Buddhist modes of think-ing, human beings are sentient beings. Sensitivity, rather than rationality, is the distinctive feature of humanity. We feel; therefore we are. Through feeling, we realize our own existence and the coexistence of other human beings, indeed birds, animals, plants and all the myriad things in the universe. Since this feeling of interconnectedness is not merely a private emotion but a sense of fellowship that is intersubjectively confirmable, it is a commonly shareable value.

In a deeper sense, sympathy is not a learned capacity but a naturally endowed quality of the heart-and-mind. It is natural to feel the suffering of others. Even if we are hardened by circumstances beyond our control and desensitized by frequent exposure to atrocities, our ability to respond to tragic events is never totally lost. Yet, one of the saddest human tragedies is the temporary loss of any sympathy toward the perceived enemy. In the case of a psychopath or a terrorist obsessed with revenge and retaliation, the victim (often the innocent victim) is so "dehumanized" that inflicting pain, suffering and death upon him or her is deemed inevitable or even desirable. It is not the absence of instrumental rationality, self-righteousness and moral indignation (of course in the most distorted forms imaginable) but the total lack of sympathy, empathy and compassion that makes the actions of such a human being so inhumanly devastating. The cultivation of sympathy, through education, as a way of recovering the original heart-and-mind endowed in human nature is essential for nurturing a global mindset of peace.

Obviously, it is naïve to believe that the cultivation of sympathy can actually combat terrorism. Yet, undeniably, politically manipulated and "religiously charged" terrorism is motivated by a firm belief that extraordinarily violent measures are necessary to right perceived wrong. Otherwise how could intelligent men and women of faith be so thoroughly "brainwashed" that they design elaborate schemes to murder innocent people by committing suicide themselves? The psychopathology, or sheer madness, underlying such desperate action is most frightening. The hatred is so intense that the ultimate suffering—death by suicide—is employed as a strategy to inflict the maximum damage. The idea of "live and let live" is inverted. Human intelligence demands that we probe deeply into the mindset of these terrorists in order to understand how they actually end up choosing cruel and dehumanizing action. Several common values are distorted and abused to justify the inevitability of such an outrageous act: sincerity, commitment, moral indignation, rationality, sacrifice, righteousness and daring; yet, sympathy, empathy and compassion for anyone considered as "other" are totally absent. These essential features of humanity are completely rejected by the tough-minded terrorists.

Without sympathy, empathy and compassion, sincerity degenerates into obsessiveness, commitment into fanaticism, moral indignation into aggressive anger, rationality into an instrument of destruction, sacrifice into massive suffering, righteousness into arrogance and daring into brutality. Humanity as sensitivity and sensibility nurtures other values so that sincerity, commitment, moral indignation, rationality, sacrifice, righteousness and daring can enrich our inner resources and strengthen our resolve to cultivate a mindset of peace through personal transformation.

## Legality and Civility

The rule of law is essential for the maintenance of order. The demand for transparency in the market economy, for public accountability in a democratic polity and for due process in civil society strongly indicates that, without the rule of law, it is difficult to assure security, good governance and the protection of rights. Yet law, as the minimum condition for orderliness, cannot in itself generate public-spiritedness or a sense of responsibility. The cultivation of a civic ethic is necessary for people who seek the fullness of life in communal harmony. Since a multiplicity of traditions guides the thoughts and actions of the world's peoples, legality without civility cannot inspire public-spiritedness. A legal system devoid of a civic ethic can easily degenerate into excessive litigiousness.

Civility complements the rule of law and provides legality with a moral base. It is the proper way to deal with fellow citizens. If positive global trends—those that enhance communication and interconnection without increasing hegemonism—help to bring about an ever-expanding connected community, civility is the key to sustaining such a process. Without civility, genuine dialogue is impossible. Civility is indispensable in intercultural communication. Our willingness to suspend judgment, to critically examine our own assumptions, to appreciate what has been said without drawing up premature conclusions, to inquire further into the relevant points and to reflect on the meaning of the interchange is congenial to the cultivation of a civic ethic.

Humanity enables us to establish a reciprocal relationship with the other; justice helps us to put our humane feelings for the other into action; and civility provides the proper form of interpersonal communication. Without civility, competition becomes a brutal task of domination and tension, and an adversarial system quickly degenerates into a hostile struggle for power. Laws in themselves may well encourage compliance, but the cultivation of civility is essential for the smooth functioning of a harmonious society. As we envision a global civil society in which the lateral relationships of all cultures, including newly emerging ones, facilitate mutual learning, hope for perpetual peace is being fostered.

The emergence of a global civil society, as reflected in the creative imagination, enthusiastic participation and dynamic activity of nongovernmental organizations at Rio (environment and development, 1992), Cairo (population, 1994), Copenhagen (social development, 1995) and Beijing (women, 1995) strongly suggests that newer players on the international scene, transcending ethnic, linguistic, cultural and religious boundaries, require new rules of the game to help negotiate a terrain replete with tension and conflict with a tolerable level of civility. We cannot depend only on clearly specified laws and regulations to guide our conduct in this unfamiliar territory. A common sense of decency and hospitality, taught in virtually all the spiritual traditions, provides a basis for dialogue and communication.

In the language of civility, diplomacy between nations is translated into politeness between individuals. Fear of the other breeds the unhealthy desire to dominate. Anger easily leads to violence and the psychology of suspicion is a major cause for aggression. While vigilance is necessary for navigating in troubled waters, civil action rather than military or legal action is the only sustainable approach to enduring interpersonal relationships. An ethic of civility is not a substitute for the rule of law, but, without the spirit of civility, law-abiding citizens can be aloof, indifferent and even rude. Civility encourages humanity, reciprocity and trust and at the same time complements legality.

## Rights and Responsibility

While rights-consciousness is essential for cultivating autonomy, independence and personal dignity, the emphasis on the idea of a freely choosing and rights-bearing individual without any sense of obligation, duty or responsibility is not congenial to social solidarity or human flourishing. Since the United Nations' 1948 Universal Declaration of Human Rights, advocacy of human rights has become a salient feature of modern consciousness. The state's advocacy of human rights is no longer confined to a handful of developed countries. Most United Nations members subscribe to some, if not all, of the international human rights agreements. Even regimes with blatant violations of human rights are compelled by public opinion to pay lip service to those rights. The spirit of our time encourages rights discourse to spread to all corners of the world and to embrace all of humanity, transcending race, gender, class, age and faith.

However, human rights have evolved from political rights to encompass economic rights and, eventually, cultural and group rights. While the original United Nations Universal Declaration of Human Rights is comprehensive in its coverage, the actual process of implementation has been painfully slow, even among nations most articulate in promoting human rights as a universal human aspiration. Although the claims that countries can have different concepts of human rights and that we ought not demand that all nations comply with universal standards of human rights are subject to criticism, how to coordinate and integrate political rights with economic, social, cultural and group rights is of vital importance for a cross-cultural dialogue.

Underlying the necessity and desirability of an international dialogue on human rights is the question of the responsibility and, by implication, duty and obligation of all dialogical partners. While rights-consciousness with its multifaceted dimensions emerged rather recently in human history, all spiritual traditions developed a mature sense of responsibility or duty-consciousness early in human civilization. Some of the criticism leveled against the human rights discourse may have been motivated by the specific desire of political leaders to underscore deference to authority as a cornerstone for stability.

It is a truism to note that countries at different stages of economic development or with different historical traditions and cultural backgrounds have different perceptions and practices of human rights. However, human rights, as a defining characteristic of modernity, must not be subject to dictatorial or authoritarian polity. Placing an equal emphasis on rights and responsibility is a balanced approach to human flourishing and an effective way of cross-cultural dialogue.

Indeed, rights without responsibility may lead to a form of self-indulgence, indicative of egocentrism at the expense of harmonious social relationships. The moral strength of rights-consciousness lies in its generalized appeal to the dignity of the individual versus the coercive power of the state. Often human rights advocates are inspired by a sense of justice not for themselves but for the marginalized and the silenced who, constrained by forces beyond their control, are incapable of defending themselves. Underlying the rights discourse is the recognition that all fellow human beings are interconnected. Implicit in the recognition is a sense of responsibility for those not fortunate enough to demand that their rights be protected. Persons with the idea of inalienable rights solely motivated by self-interest easily turn out to be egoists.

The principle deduced from the above is that the privilege of rights entails responsibility. Are those who are more powerful and influential more obligated for the well-being of the collectivity variously defined, from the family to the global community? Several countries have specified nonjudiciable rights, such as job security and economic prosperity, in their constitutions. Unlike freedoms of speech, assembly and religion, however, one cannot demand that the government grant nonjudiciable rights as a matter of principle. They are, nevertheless, legitimate aspirations of ordinary citizens that, by and large, responsible governments try to attain. Again, it is highly advisable that the beneficiaries of a particular society assume the responsibility for its weak and underprivileged. Similarly, do the "winners" of the global market economy cultivate a duty-consciousness consonant with their power, influence and accessibility to technology, information, ideas and material resources?

## D. Wisdom

Humanity and trust underlie the common values. Without them, liberty/justice, rationality/sympathy, legality/civility and rights/responsibility will not have the wholesome ethical environment in which to become fully realized. Yet, the acquisition of common values requires a kind of personal intelligence that has been the focus of philosophical reflection since the dawn of human civilization. The Socratic ideal to "know thyself" entails the spiritual exercise and moral self-cultivation, the humanist way of learning, to be fully human. While intelligence signifies the ability to learn from experience, to acquire and retain knowledge and to use the faculty of reason in solving problems, it is through personal intelligence as wisdom that human beings have survived and flourished. In light of the grave dangers that seriously threaten our viability as a species, the need for wisdom is compelling.

Wisdom connotes holistic understanding, profound self-knowledge, a long-term perspective, common sense and good judgment. A spark of inspiration may elucidate an aspect of the world's situation, but a comprehensive grasp of the human condition requires continuous education. A fragmented approach to learning is inadequate. Personal knowledge, the kind of experiential self-awareness that is both communal and critical, can only be cultivated through persistent effort. If we go after short-term gains at the expense of long-term benefits, we may be smart, but never wise. Although thinking in a long-term perspective implies a prophetic vision, wisdom, far from being speculative thought, always brings about concrete results. The ability to take a variety of factors into account in making judgments is a sign of wisdom. While healthy dialogue requires suspension of preconceived opinions, the nonjudgmental attitude does not mean the absence of good judgment. The judgment of the wise is measured and balanced; it is the middle path transcending opinionated extremes.

Advances in science and technology have so significantly broadened our horizons and deepened our awareness of the world around us that many feel that the wisdom of the great religions and philosophical traditions is irrelevant to our modern education. Surely, globalization has greatly expanded the data, information and knowledge available for our use and consumption, but it has also substantially undermined the time-honored ways of learning, especially the traditional means of acquiring wisdom. We cannot confuse data with information, information with knowledge and knowledge with wisdom; we need to learn how to become wise, not merely informed and knowledgeable. There are three essential ways to acquire wisdom worth special attention in our information age.

First is the art of listening. Listening requires more patience and receptivity than seeing. Without patience, we may listen but fail to grasp the message, let alone the subtle meaning therein; without receptivity, the message will not register in the inner recesses of our hearts and minds even if we manage to capture what is said. Through deep listening, we genuinely encounter others. Indigenous peoples, for example, can teach us how to listen not only to one another but also to the voice of nature. Only through deep listening will we truly comprehend what is communicated through the ear.

The second is face-to-face communication. Talking directly with another is the most common and simplest way to communicate, but it is also the most challenging and rewarding. Conversation over the telephone, or using even more sophisticated electronic devices, is no substitute for a face-to-face talk. A partner is required for this kind of communication. Face-to-face communication is the most enduring method of human interaction and, in the last analysis, the most authentic way of transmitting values. If it is relegated to the background, there is little chance that we can become wise.

The art of listening and face-to-face communication are the indispensable ways to access the third timeless way of learning: the cumulative wisdom of the elders. Precisely because we are exposed to so much data, information and knowledge in the modern world, our need to acquire wisdom is more urgent than ever. The wisdom of the great religious and philosophical traditions teaches us how to be fully human. The cumulative wisdom of the elders refers to the art of living embodied in the thoughts and actions of a given society's exemplars. Only through exemplary teaching, teaching by example rather than by words, can we learn to be fully human. We cannot afford to cut ourselves off from the spiritual resources that make our life meaningful. We emulate those who exemplify the most inspiring ways of being fully human in our society, not only with our brain, but also with our heart and mind, indeed our entire body. This form of embodied learning cannot be done by simulation alone. Understandably, language, history, literature, classics, philosophy, religion and cultural anthropology—subjects in the liberal arts education—help us to acquire wisdom and are never outdated.

Learning to be fully human involves character building rather than the acquisition of knowledge or the internalization of skills. Cultural as well as technical competence are required to function well in the contemporary world. Ethical as well as cognitive intelligence is essential for personal growth; without the former, the moral fabric of society will be undermined. Spiritual ideas and exercises as well as adequate material conditions are crucial for the well-being of the human community. Cultural competence is also highly desirable. Even if we do not possess literacy, a sense of history, a taste for literature or a rudimentary knowledge of the classics, we can still live up to the basic expectations of citizenship, but our participation in our nation's civic life will be impoverished. Ethical intelligence is necessary for social solidarity. Spiritual ideas and exercises are not dispensable luxuries for the leisure class; they are an integral part of the life of the mind that gives a culture a particular character and a distinct ethos.

The values specified above are selective rather than comprehensive. Acting in accordance with these values is necessary for an effective and enriching dialogue among civilizations; these values can also be cultivated through the actual process of the dialogue. They are common values that have been articulated by all spiritual traditions in different contexts and historical situations. These values can be taught through example, story sharing, religious preaching, ethical instruction and, most of all, dialogue.

The ideas in this chapter can be shown in a simple diagram with two propositions: (1) Globalization may lead to faceless homogenization that is ignorant about differences and arrogant about hegemonic power; through dialogue, it may also lead to a genuine sense of global community. (2) The quest for identity may lead to pernicious exclusion, with ethnocentric bigotry and exclusivist violence; through dialogue, it may also lead to an authentic way of global communication and a real respect for diversity.

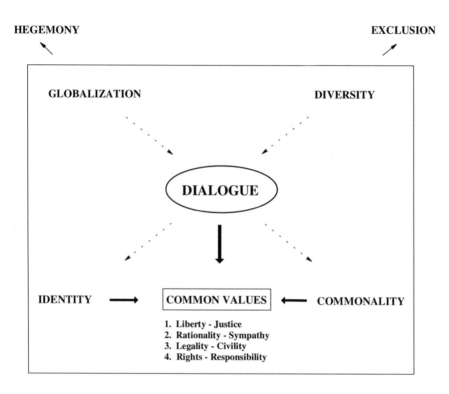

Figure 2

# CHAPTER 3

*A New Paradigm
of Global Relations*

# A New Paradigm of Global Relations

## A. Introduction

### *The Old Paradigm: Its Key Elements*

The theory of the "clash of civilizations" was an attempt to reinvent a new enemy for those, and there were many, who felt the unbearable burden of being without one. Not much different was the attempt to declare "the end of history," for it proclaimed the victory of one side over the other. They were not theories for the beginning of a new era, but rather theories that concluded the old. They were inherently germane to the old paradigm: the paradigm of "either-or," of "us and them," of exclusion.

Exclusion was and is the core element of a paradigm that many would say had survived for millennia. As borders were elevated to the order of nationhood, the concept of "enemy" became an indispensable ingredient of the same old paradigm; a convenient one as well, for "enemy" is a tool of power management.

With few exceptions, most notably the great religious and moral leaders, we have not had leaders who could lead without "enemy." They succeeded in changing the paradigm at an individual level, but they did not change it at a social level because society continued to be ruled by governance through exclusion. The significance of those few exceptions is that their appeal to the hearts and minds of individuals might be seen as a sign of aspiration toward a paradigm of inclusion, though one is not yet in existence.

The world of the old paradigm had many boundaries; it was predicated on geographic exclusion first and foremost. There were many other boundaries as well: religious, cultural, racial, tribal, gender. Another characteristic of this old paradigm was its interpretation of the concept of diversity: diversity as a synonym of threat, if not of enmity. If diversity were carried through in its negative perception, one would quickly reach "demonization of the other," deepen the divide and build even higher walls. The tragedy of it all is that we are not talking about centuries ago; we are talking about times and places in our own lifetimes.

"Demonization of the other" seems to go hand in hand with "ignorance of the other"; in fact, they may be directly proportional. Exclusion, boundaries, enmity and demonization are all fed in different ways by ignorance. It was not an accident that the leaders of yesteryear wanted a monopoly of knowledge, and it is not an accident that our past history is full of examples of prevarication of knowledge, destruction of the tools of knowledge and refusal to learn. At the very base of all evils of the old paradigm is the very arrogance of ignorance that alone can lead to the highest level of the arrogance of power. It was the paradigm that "might makes right" on which many ideologies were built and many empires tried to survive.

## The Undermining of the Old Paradigm

It is unrealistic to state that such a complex paradigm comes to an end at a given point in time and a new one begins. In fact, much of the old paradigm of "us vs. them" still exists and prevails in the minds of many and in the acts of some. But it seems to us that much is happening to indicate that a new paradigm has already begun to develop, and that its seeds already exist. Our attempt will be to encourage and nurture these seeds.

An essential condition of the old paradigm is the concept of boundaries of any kind, and of the necessity of exclusion. What has really undermined the old paradigm is any development that has begun to create a borderless reality, be it perceived or factual. One could argue that the universal institutions that developed in the twentieth century, most notably the United Nations, were the first attempts, conscious or unconscious, to challenge the old paradigm. It was that expression of universality that first conveyed the sense of a global reality beyond the divided and fragmented one. By definition, the United Nations was born with the objective of creating a sense of oneness of the international community, and therefore it began chipping away at the mentality of borders and boundaries.

The set of institutions that followed, both at the political and at the economic level, and the various United Nations agencies on an issue-driven level, represented in their very conception a step beyond diversity as synonym of enmity or diversity as a threat. The universality of those institutions carried with it the unavoidable requirement of equality at both the macro and the micro level of society, further chipping away at the very concept of "us and them," which is so essential to the old paradigm. It matters not that these ideas have not been completely implemented during the last century, or fifty, or forty or thirty years. What does matter is that they have begun to erode the validity of the concept of diversity as a threat in its racial, religious, ethnic, gender and cultural dimensions.

In a larger sense, the development of international law has added to the erosion of the old paradigm, since international law is based on the recognition of rules and rights applicable to all, irrespective of any divide. The double standard that has been employed in applying the rules and behaviors that we claim are universal, however, has created new divisions. This double standard may well have been the original sin of the old paradigm, a sin that we have unabashedly continued to commit.

The emergence of borderless trends in society is further eroding the old paradigm, be they economic and financial globalization; real-time communication; global networking among elements of civil society; ecological concerns; vulnerability to contagious diseases; or unprecedented levels of migration and creation of "diaspora" communities.

Modern coalition-building is increasingly becoming issue-based across traditional boundaries. Both great globalizers—the large corporations—and anti-globalizers—"the people of Seattle"—are producing the same effect on the old paradigm. They are both undermining it because neither exists within traditional boundaries. Both sides of the barricade are serving the same purpose. The nation-state remains, of course, the glue of international society, though one of its elements—namely, borders—has become more and more porous.

## The Germination of the New Paradigm

As we have tried to underline the elements that are undermining the old paradigm, we also wish to identify those seeds of the new paradigm already growing at the macro level. Global issues exist that require global solutions. They can only be dealt with by the entire community of nations jointly. Global climate issues are perhaps the most self-evident indication that a new paradigm is in the making. Another is the linkage between women's human rights and seemingly intractable global problems, which was addressed in the worldwide conference in Beijing in 1995. At the Congress of Vienna in 1815, one could hardly have heard any reference to "global issues," and even less to "global solutions." Today, such a reality is commonly accepted.

Coalition-building across borders by civil society's actors has brought about informal fora where cross-border issues are addressed and solutions are offered and sought irrespective of the traditional institutional framework. At the micro level today, the voice of small groups, even the voice of one individual, has a chance to be heard by many and to receive feedback from many as never before in the history of society. Those who have access to real-time communication, which is a two-way street, have an opportunity to get their message across.

The Truth and Reconciliation Commission in South Africa and the International Criminal Court may well represent a qualitative change of paradigm challenging previously unassailable concepts of law. First, they have given value to the concept of repentance and forgiveness in the management of the affairs of society. Second, they have introduced the concept of individual responsibility at the level of the *res publica,* at the level of the state and, indeed, of international relations. In fact, within the framework of the International Criminal Court, we have seen the very concept of individual responsibility applied not only to the vanquished but also to the victors. Third, issues that were considered to be within the boundaries of the state are now scrutinized by the international community. Individuals are now answerable to international law, whereas previously only states were the responsible parties. While not necessarily usurping state authority, international tribunals are dealing directly with certain crimes committed by individuals within a state.

Perhaps as never before, the last ten years have ushered in the hope for developments that previously seemed impossible. The unthinkable, even at the macro level of international society, has become possible. We have seen changes occur that were simply unpredictable, providing not only a paradigmatic change but also, and most importantly, hope where there was none, and the opportunity for new visions and developments. Impossible situations have been reversed; more justice has been dispensed. At the same time more prejudice, bigotry, discrimination, racism and even genocide have re-emerged. The emergence of hope has opened the door to more demand for justice and, accordingly, to the possibility for more victims of injustice to believe that their aspirations will one day be met.

New coalitions have provided and are providing unprecedented avenues to meet the hopes and even the dreams of young generations. Although cynicism still exists, international civil society is taking on challenges that would have seemed impossible fifty years ago. Today they receive a degree of support and commitment at the level of individuals across borders unthinkable only two generations ago. Can we speak of moral courage and a larger sense of solidarity, unofficial solidarity at least, among unofficial groups across boundaries in order to pursue objectives that may have seemed at different times just unreachable? Entire industrial sectors, powerful sectors, have been forced to take heed of the requests and the demands of much less powerful coalitions that have shown a determination and an ability to create wider and wider public interest. Today, oppressed minorities, nations without their own institutions, victims of AIDS, victims of violence against women and trafficking in human beings and child soldiers have hope that the international community will respond in favor of justice. At any other time in history, these victims, voiceless, would have been trapped by anonymity.

Another example of the germination of the new paradigm is what we call the "hope for justice," for finding solutions to disputes and conflicts. The classic debate between peace and justice may not yet be resolved. However, a more realistic attitude is taking hold, namely, the recognition of the hope for justice as an indispensable component of solutions to disputes and conflicts. In a way, expectations may have been lowered, but the requirement of a hope for justice has become stronger.

### The New Paradigm

The new paradigm that we believe is emerging and that we hope will be fostered is, simply, a paradigm of inclusion by necessity and by choice. It is by necessity because of the global dimension of problems, dangers, challenges and solutions, as well as because of interdependence among all. It is by choice because in an age without existential enemies at the level of state and an increasingly borderless reality, we benefit more from inclusion than from exclusion. It is by choice because of the emerging consensus on the dignity of the human person, instead of the acceptance that "might makes right." To a large extent, we are moving more and more towards a reality where either we all win together or we all lose together. It may be that the emergence of this new paradigm has made it more difficult to resolve conflicts, for the price of a solution that involves compromise has become higher and the readiness to accept that "might makes right" has become weaker.

Today one can see a movement not only toward competition in a free market but also toward fairness in competition. Systems of regulations, antitrust laws, environmental protections, fair labor laws and gradual adjustments are examples of this move towards fairness. At the same time, perceiving diversity as a threat, as enmity—a major characteristic of the old paradigm—still persists, and examples continue to emerge in different parts of the world. However, the necessity and choice of looking at diversity as an element of growth and betterment—a characteristic of the emerging new paradigm—is equally present. While there continue to be anti-immigration demonstrations and even violence throughout Europe—a manifestation of the old paradigm—European Union (EU) studies already show that thirty-five million new adult immigrants into the EU will be needed by 2025 for the economic growth of that region.

While the old paradigm still demonizes the enemy, the new paradigm is transforming the enemy into a competitor, an opponent, a partner. To be sure, the many examples of violent enmity that have erupted over the last ten years may well have been last-ditch attempts by those who feared the coming of the new paradigm and, more specifically, the loss of a traditional enemy. For they were and they still are unable to manage and, indeed, to rule without an enemy. The new paradigm requires leaderships to base their governance on positive values, constructive contributions and eagerness to include rather than govern through exclusion and, in some cases, even rule through a perpetual enemy.

In a way, the new paradigm requires a new kind of leader. If there is an enemy that confronts the new leader, it comes from within his or her own community, his or her own group, even himself or herself, and not from outside. His or her greatness is the consequence of the positive values that he or she offers, not of the negative that he or she purports to fight. The new leader's vision is anchored in a society where participation is wide and many voices are heard, where the door is open to new channels for that participation and for new voices to have a role. This vision is one where institutions are not the remnants of the past, but are open to be reshaped and remodeled. It is one that looks at a future not yet defined; where ideas are not feared but welcomed and discussed; where a new balance between the dignity of each individual and the wisdom of traditions is found.

Perhaps most of all, the new paradigm allows for individuals who conceive of their public service as a temporary honor in a professional life, rather than as a permanent occupation. These will be leaders who will "resign their commissions" even when asked to stay. Most of all, these will be leaders who feel their institutional responsibility equal to their personal, individual responsibility. This is a new paradigm where both institutions and individuals will have roles, and where neither will overshadow the other. For institutions do not exist without individuals, do not even think without individuals; and individuals can hardly achieve much without the structures provided by institutions. In fact, it is a paradigm where any individual may potentially become a leader. Can we aspire to leaders who lead without "enemy"?

> *The ruler rules with virtue, not force.*
>
> — *Confucius*

## B. The Elements of the New Paradigm

The processes of globalization are giving birth to a new paradigm of global relations: equal footing; re-assessment of the "enemy"; dispersion of power; stakeholding; individual responsibility; and issue-driven alignments. The current reality is a mosaic of the old and the new. The elements of the new paradigm are already there, but to a certain extent we are blinded by the old paradigm, which prevents us from seeing what is emerging. Of course, this is how human societies evolve: the border between the old and the new, between yesterday and today, is seldom precise.

### *Equal Footing*

It seems to us that the deepest meaning of dialogue is an instrument through which a shift of paradigm can take place. In this respect, dialogue requires the rejection of "diversity as a threat" and the acceptance of the "other" as equal.

Equal footing seems to be defined at a minimum as a situation where each voice can be heard and is given a chance and a framework by which to be heard, and at a maximum as *equal participation*. Equal footing, however, is not to be seen as an act of charity by the stronger to the weaker. Even the weaker possesses a bargaining chip, and that is the expression of support for legitimacy that it can provide to the stronger.

Equal footing implies equal respect for the dignity of each actor on the international scene as well as in a national setting. The aspiration to equality and fairness is not new. It has been pursued by many at different times, both at the institutional and at the civil society level, both locally and internationally. The aspiration to equality reflects the universal desire for freedom, and rejection of dominance by the stronger over the weaker. In the context of nations where there is respect for the rule of law, a degree of equality is provided. At the international level, attempts at domination have been justified by the need for security and, in some cases, even by survival. Where a threat to existence is no longer real, and where countries have learned by necessity or choice to need each other and to benefit from each other, the aspiration towards equal footing is more achievable.

Interdependence, whether it is at the level of economics, migrations, diseases, terrorism or art, has brought closer the possibility of achieving a sense of equal footing. The reciprocal need for each other in different forms at the international level has never been so self-evident and has never been recognized by so many. Many, of course, have not yet done so; but they are those who have elevated to an ideology the sense of exclusion and the fear of others that can derive from a sense of insecurity in one's own beliefs.

Dialogue brings with it equal footing, whether consciously or unconsciously, as it is a process by which we accept, as much as we want to be accepted. We include, as much as we want to be included. We listen, as much as we want to be listened to. In these terms, dialogue can perhaps eventually usher in a new paradigm of global relations because it challenges the old paradigm. To the extent that real democracy is measured by the degree of respect for minorities rather than by the rule of the majority, even at the global level dialogue can be a framework where the weakest is accorded the privilege to be listened to, and where the strongest finds it necessary to explain its case to others.

There seems to be no question that instinctively, the introduction of the concept of equal footing on the international scene may appear to be an idealistic and unachievable goal, particularly as we emerge from a decade where states have resorted to "might" quite often. These cases of "might" over "right," however, have engendered a reaction that over time is becoming stronger: a demand for right and justice in louder and louder voices. We may have seen cases over the last ten years of "unjust" peace. We are very likely going to see fewer and fewer of those cases, as the choice of temporary peace over justice was easier to make under the old paradigm, but is much harder to make in the new emerging one. The prominence of peace at any price over justice was more attuned to a paradigm of exclusion, of "might makes right," and of victor and vanquished, where the concept of "enemy" is king. As the new paradigm emerges, the preeminence of peace at any price over justice seems to be losing some of its luster. It may take longer, and indeed there may be more pain, but it seems that more and more people are prepared to place a higher value on justice or the hope for justice than on peace at any cost than only twenty or ten years ago. As much as the last decade has been characterized by many examples of the use of force over law, and of the coming into being of the one super-power, the demand for equal footing throughout the world has become louder and stronger.

While the reality of difference in power and size and eco-nomic weight of various parties will not easily change, even if the mindset were to change, we can find encourage-ment in the fact that the rule of law is prevailing in more countries now than in past decades. In those societies, the weak find a way to lead a full life under the protection of commonly accepted norms and behaviors. In different forms, we have moved toward the search for equal foot-ing, whether it is in local or international society. In fact, the very need for this aspiration is not being challenged any longer; more so, both at the local and at the interna-tional level, what prevails is the attempt to claim the existence of an equal footing situation, even when this is actually not so.

Globalization may well have offered the possibility for the stronger to pass on their own messages around the globe in a deeper way than ever before. It has also unavoidably opened the possibility for the weaker to take advantage of information technology, to have his or her own message reach the stronger as never before. Even more, globaliza-tion has carried with it interdependence, and it is interdependence that has brought about the possibility for the weaker to affect the stronger. We have seen so not only at the economic and financial levels, but also at the political and social levels. It is the two-way street of inter-dependence, though recognizably imbalanced, that has paradoxically increased even the chances for equal footing.

Interdependence may not have been planned, and the move toward more equal participation may not have been on the wish list of all, but this is also one of the consequences of a more interconnected world. In 1898, the mighty British pound would hardly have been weakened by the collapse of the currency of any of the British colonies. However, in 1997, the collapse of the Thai baht sent its ripples throughout five continents, and began what will be remembered as the financial crisis of the end of the decade.

Many less powerful countries owed their influence in the past, as in the present, to their size, their natural resources or their population. Today, however, we can add a new series of countries that owe their influence and their profile in the world to their knowledge, their contribution to the wider world's knowledge and their ability to use knowledge that comes from others in a more efficient manner. A number of such entities come surely to mind, and their role in this world is certainly not the consequence of demography or geography, commodities or military power. It is the outcome of the information society. Singapore and Hong Kong have taken a leading role in the acquisition, use and proliferation of knowledge in technology. Their size is not an inhibiting factor; their ability clearly is crucial. While we cannot claim this is so everywhere, the very existence of knowledge centers highly regarded throughout the world, both in developing and in Organization for Economic Co-operation and Development (OECD) countries, stands to prove that equal footing is not a figment of imagination.

Indeed, it would appear that over the last several years the role and profile of countries is the result of their ability to project and to use knowledge rather than their military or geographical size. Finland, Norway, Singapore, South Korea and Chile are examples in different fields in economics, diplomacy or technology. In the world that valued only labor and commodities, this could hardly have occurred. In a world where ideas and knowledge began to be equally relevant, if not more, this has become possible.

Globalization has made it possible for dialogue to become more real than ever, for access and control of bandwidth, transponders, frequencies and fiber optics is already dispersed throughout the world. Those channels of communication are by no means equally distributed, but they are no longer the monopoly of one country or one set of countries. Communication satellites have been launched by more countries than those possessing nuclear weapons, and the waves and the frequencies can be occupied and invaded not only by institutionalized power centers but also by groups as varied as NGOs or terrorist organizations and even as small as one individual. Technology access and access to scientific discoveries, both in chemistry and in physics, have made knowledge simply more accessible than one could ever have dreamed only fifty years ago. And this, of course, is for better or for worse.

The trend for stronger nations to treat weaker ones on an equal footing is fostered by both equality in vulnerability and, perhaps less so, equality in opportunity. We can all see the emergence of new and at times sinister issues on the global agenda. The fight against terrorism; HIV/AIDS; the regulation of new technologies such as human cloning, genetic transformation and bioengineering; copyrights on intellectual property; anti-narcotic rules; disease control; and control of interference in the computing systems of institutions, countries, parties and organizations are only some of the dimensions that require for their success the full cooperation of all members of international society. Accordingly, even the smallest needs to be brought in, and even the smallest may have an important contribution to make. In the fight against contagious disease, the coalition against it is only as strong as its weakest member, which means in fact that the weakest member of the coalition has power and responsibility. In dealing with the effects of foot and mouth disease or the rise in sea level, which may wipe out a whole economy or even a whole state, it is the cooperation of each and every member through dialogue that is indispensable. If even one person fails to cooperate with contagious disease prevention or treatment, then all others are at risk. All of these threats require the allegiance of all members of the international community to common rules or a set of norms. Indeed, the ability to face these threats can and will be successful only if the weakest commits to that challenge as well. It is this equality in vulnerability that stimulates dialogue. Equality in vulnerability is also the direct consequence of interdependence in many, many levels. It is this interdependence that has transformed "the threat" into "global threat."

A dialogue across divides, across borders and across cultures is a dialogue that provides dignity, affords respect and results in allegiance to norms, rules and principles of common behavior that those who do not believe that "might makes right" find natural to embrace. So the case for equal footing in international affairs in the year 2001 can be made more strongly than in 1981, for as certain key international actors have become stronger, they have also become more vulnerable. We would like to suggest that dialogue, as a way of interaction, will foster democratization of the international system, recognizing the incredible differences that continue to exist in terms of economic capabilities, political power and military might. Dialogue introduces a dimension of equal footing; it cannot and does not, however, change the factual reality of power. It may open the door to new and different roles for each of the members of the international community. The key remains that the voice of each be heard.

Here lies, possibly, the strength of the weaker and the ability of the weaker to further achieve equal footing. The adherence to common rules of behavior and common norms requires an act of decision by each individual member of the international community, no matter how small. The acceptance of those norms becomes for the weaker, therefore, on one side a necessity and on the other a higher moral pulpit from which to speak.

### Re-assessment of the "Enemy"

These recognizable threats to the international system, however we choose to define it, have to a large extent already begun to affect the way many look at the "enemy."

It may be presumptuous to sketch here a paradigm of relations where the concept of enemy is no more. We may have to concede that we have hardly had any leaders who could lead without enemies, for "the enemy" is first and foremost a management tool for power. Of course, we have had some spectacular changes over the last fifty years, at least in some regions of the world, which illustrate how we can go from a situation of enmity to one of friendship. The European continent, which for centuries has been bloodied by wars, with the so-called traditional enmity between France and Germany, has seen a transformation that was unforeseeable only fifty years ago. The Western European countries not only have gone from enmity to cooperation and alliance but also have moved to an integration of values, economies, finance and even politics that now makes the enmity relationship of the past unthinkable. It is also significant that those structures and those institutions have been taken as an example, with due changes, by other groups of states, most recently by the members of the African Union.

Some may suggest that the transition from a society where the concept of enemy is an inherent component to an "enemy-less" society may well be too big a jump, even from an idealistic point of view. But the reality of globalization and the desire for dialogue may open the door to the reexamination of the concept of enemy and to a definition of the new enemy.

The threats just outlined are to a different extent true for every society, every culture, in every latitude. They are not unique to a particular nation, to a particular culture, to any particular people. Perhaps what we are really talking about is no longer individual enemies for individual countries, but a multifaceted enemy for all. The spreading of contagious disease, terrorism, weapons of mass destruction, unrestricted dissemination of small weapons or poverty all represent different faces of an "enemy" for the entire human race. In a new paradigm based on the reality of common threats to the entire human community, the real "enemy" is no longer an individual, a state, a culture or a religion and most of all, it is no longer a specific "enemy" for a specific country or people. If the enemy is common, it follows that fighting against it requires unanimity.

The recognized and recognizable need for a joint struggle by all members of the international community against any one of these threats further strengthens the point that even the weakest member of the community needs to be brought into alignment for the struggle. If a successful dialogue is a process by which diversity is no longer perceived as a threat, it follows that a successful dialogue may undermine one of the strongest rationales for the concept of "enemy" itself. Unavoidably throughout history, the "enemy" has been associated with the "other," with "that which is different." To a large extent, it has also been associated with ignorance of the other.

Targeting the dialogue, therefore, on the concept of diversity represents a threat for those who need to feed themselves on the existence of "enemy." It is very likely that we will see among opponents of dialogue those who need to demonize an enemy instead of providing rational arguments or positive incentives to advance their vested interests. We expect no understanding for dialogue by these centers of power and influence, for dialogue and abandoning the perception of diversity as a threat would undermine their cohesive power. In a way, this would be the test of those who profess dialogue merely in words and those who pursue dialogue in deeds; between those who need an enemy to be who they are, and those who simply are, because of what they offer in terms of rationality and positive values. The concept of "enemy" has traditionally been seen as a threat to our own very existence. In an era of interdependence, and despite September 11, 2001, it is more likely that "the enemy" is not someone who will have the power to destroy us, but someone who can compete or be an antagonist. In a way, the terms "enemy" and "war" are used only in marginal cases, and they refer only to extreme situations. More likely, when speaking of relations among countries, for instance, we include terms like "competitor," "opponent," and "adversary," nouns that do not contain the message of existential annihilation. In some cases, old enemies have become competitive partners, and in some cases they have become full partners. In the field of economics, we hardly find the word "enemy," but we often find the word "competitor." In the social dimension, we have gone from the concept of class enemies to that of stakeholders, though not necessarily shareholders. In the last several years, we even have seen wars fought among countries that did not define their adversary with the term "enemy."

We are not, however, only speaking of a change in terminology; we are probably witnessing a very unconscious acceptance that the total "enemy" is more and more difficult to identify. Yes, there are still those who will be able to define it for us in physical and time dimensions. And it is also true that we have all witnessed the invention of new enemies during the past decade. Can we call "ethnic conflict" one fought between individuals who until the day before were living in the same quarters, and in fact even intermarrying? Is this not the "invention of an enemy"? But while these cases, as extreme as they were, have stuck in our recent memory, it is also true that in terms of numbers, "peoples at war" are but a small minority of the six billion human beings who populate our planet. Many more are "fighting" the plagues of diseases, of drug abuse, of criminality, than those who are involved in armed conflict against the "enemy" of yesteryear.

There are those who, deprived of the "comfort" of having an enemy, keep trying to invent one. And the latest seems to be globalization. To be sure, globalization is seen by some as an opponent not of their physical existence, but of that concept of human solidarity that is boundary-less and that is becoming the banner of many, not only in the social and economic dimension but also in the environmental, ethical and medical spheres. Many are very comfortable with a reality where competition exists, but not enmity; where stakeholding exists, but not enmity; and indeed where partnership exists, but not enmity. But then there are those who ask for more. They ask for human solidarity beyond and above the rules of economics, of local interest or even of global interests. Human solidarity is probably a level above partnership, for it finds its justification and aspirations in the very concept of fellowship of the human species.

In a way, those who today represent in the eyes of many the world of globalization (the Bretton Woods institutions, the multinational corporations, the leaders of major powers), as well as those who meet in the streets to protest where these gatherings take place, do not belong to two different worlds, nor to two different eras; they are part of the same evolution away from the concept of "enemy."

The institutional leaders, the corporate leaders, the political leaders, are very much in favor of a world that has no enemy, for they are the first ones to embrace the concept of competitor or of adversary or of partner over that of enemy. They are the front line of globalization interpreted as the new system. The protestors, the horizontal alliances of NGOs and individuals that have met from Seattle to Prague, from Stockholm to Genoa, and so forth, are also against the concept of "enemy." They are just running further ahead and faster; they are claiming—unless they fall into a new protectionism of a sort, and thus feed more exclusion—that competition is not enough, and that more is needed in order to reach that level of "enemy-lessness," for human solidarity is not seen as being satisfied by competition alone. It seems that the protestors of globalization are saying that competition still includes a degree of enmity under a different name. This cannot be reconciled with the ultimate demands for human solidarity, the only level of "enemy-less" society to which they can honestly aspire.

In fact, it is not only human solidarity, it is the request for equity, for fairness, for justice that has been thrown in the face of the institutional world, be it public or private. All this is happening in the aftermath of—or, in some cases, during a transition from—an era where the word "enemy" was so popular to one in which the word "enemy" will be fading away. The fact is that even when institutions and the institutional world move, they proceed at a slower pace than the younger generation would like. Institutions and the institutional world are the products of a previous generation; the new one, understandably, will ask for more. The supporters of globalization and those who seem superficially to oppose it belong to the same new era, one that has refused the concept of "enemy" and moved to somewhere between adversary, competitor, partner and human solidarity. They cover a gamut that is wide, but they are on the same side of the barricade, the one where qualitatively we have begun to make a step in the direction of going beyond the perception that diversity is a threat.

It is, of course, too early to claim that we have reached a state of governance without enemy, for in many societies this has not yet happened. But it is true that in many others, the enemy of yesteryear has become the partner of today. The horizontal cooperation across borders at the level of civil societies on the basis of common interest, as well as common sense, has brought together groups that found in regional cooperation a better answer than only national cooperation. The success of regional associations, be they for commercial, sectoral or security purposes, has made acceptable to so many that cooperating with your neighbor is intrinsically good. The exceptions, of course, exist and persist. Cooperating with a neighbor has triumphed in different degrees from Europe to Southeast Asia to Latin

America. In the process, these developments have eliminated in the minds of many the perception that our neighbor is potentially an enemy; in fact, they have fostered the perception that the enemy is potentially a partner.

The old paradigm motto, that alliances may vary but the interests of states do not, seems to carry less and less weight as interdependence deepens, and more and more groups and people see the benefit not only of cooperation with one's neighbor but also of horizontal cooperation with similar groups in different countries near or far. The existence of environmental, human rights, women's and human solidarity NGOs has further chipped away at the perception of enemy and the need for enemy—in fact, at the wisdom of having an enemy.

In many countries of the world, young people would have a hard time quickly answering the question, "Who is your enemy?" Of course, major exceptions still prevail, and we are all aware of them, but no longer can we say that an individual would wake up in the morning and be fully aware of who his enemy is. As we have just outlined above, the nature of the threat in many cases has changed, and is no longer embodied in one person, one state, one religion or one race. This qualitative evolution in redefining the nature of the threat is the first step in the direction of a society where the classic concept of "enemy" has been severely undermined.

While governance through "enemy" is indeed the easiest of them all, in a world where autarky or national "self-sufficiency" has become a synonym of poverty, it may be easier to see that we are moving toward a new kind of governance. We still may be far away from governance through human solidarity at the global level, but we have made significant steps forward in that direction already. Civil society, crisscrossing the world, has connected individuals with the same concerns across boundaries of many kinds. Perhaps the recognition of our own vulnerability in front of terrorism and overwhelming natural and environmental threats has helped us to go beyond the need for an enemy. Perhaps the advance of knowledge has enfranchised many more out of the isolationism of ignorance that has always fed into fear and, accordingly, into the perception of enemy.

In our lifetime, we have not only seen old enemies being reconciled, in some cases becoming partners, in some cases even becoming allies, but have also seen the ability of some to go beyond the baggage of history and, most surprisingly, to join hands in a process not only of redefining the enemy but also of forgiving the enemy. These examples are more significant for having achieved something that surely many in the past would have considered impossible, as "it was not done before." That impossibility was to transform an historical "enemy" into today's "partner" or even "ally."

These examples prove not only the ability of those countries to grow, but also, most importantly, the ability of those peoples to show that even what was never done before can actually be done. In our conversations, two cases came up more frequently than others: the historic enmity between France and Germany transformed today not only into partnerships and alliances but even into friendship; and the South African Truth and Reconciliation Commission. Others could also be recalled here—for instance, the new relationship between Vietnam and the United States. Not only was the "enemy" redefined, but also and most importantly, what these examples proved is that history continues to change and does not have to repeat itself over and over again. Those who insist on repeating the refrain of the immutable character of human nature, the immutable interest of states and the hatred of peoples through generations have been proved wrong by reality, by the deeds of those who believed in the possibility of doing what was never done before. This is the world in which we are now living, and the reason why we found courage and inspiration and optimism. Today's events, despite the many examples to the contrary, prove that the hatred that has been at the origin of thousands of years of enmity can actually be brought to an end, and that determinism in history can only be used by those who are so lazy, or worse, that they have no courage to begin a new dawn for their children.

We thus have good reason to believe that a new paradigm can realistically be based on a transformation of the concept of enemy into competitor, perhaps friend. It is time to accept that when something is not being done in human society, it is because we do not want to do it, or because the generation that is charged with doing it is simply unable to do it. We must then accept that we have failed, but our successors may succeed where we failed. The failure of one generation cannot be construed as the failure of future generations, as much as it would be convenient for those who have failed to believe so. For the diehards hanging on to the concept of enemy, there may be one consolation: yes, there are still many who are abusing history and human nature as a justification for their enmity; yes, it is true that it is very hard to see a time when we will move from "governance through enemy" to "governance through human solidarity." Perhaps to those diehards, the only message we can pass on is to look hard and deep; and if they want at all cost to find one enemy to fight for the next generation, they may not have to go very far: it is their inability to transcend diversity as a threat. It is intolerance that they harbor; it is intolerance that they should fight. Is the "last enemy of the twenty-first century" intolerance?

### Dispersion of Power

We have seen elements of the old paradigm vividly appearing in the demonstrations on the streets of the cities where international summit meetings take place. They are the demonization of "the other," of the "enemy," that some demonstrators have projected when they voice their disapproval of the G-8 meetings, of the WTO meetings, of the World Bank meetings. In doing so, the more extreme groups have joined the ranks of those who needed a new enemy; in a vague manner, they have devised one and have targeted it. The extreme fringes, therefore, are not a new phenomenon, as they represent yet another group who needs an enemy. The majority, however, of those demonstrators have proved how power is being dispersed in our modern world; their very presence was a recognition that the demonstrators represented a voice that could not be ignored. One could say that a new power center had come to the surface.

A few years earlier, an unelected organization—Greenpeace—challenged the activities of a major oil company in Nigeria as at variance with fairness, justice and the human dignity of some of the local population and as the cause of serious environmental degradation. An opinion movement was mobilized across borders that found strength in various groups in many countries, thus creating a horizontal alliance of sorts. The oil company had to consider its image, not to speak of its sales, in many of these countries and alter its activities. It had to pay heed. The pressure that came from an unelected yet grassroots organization was strong enough to be reckoned with.

Power is more dispersed than it has ever been. No longer concentrated in the halls of government or a few major financial centers, power has been spread out in the hands of many groups and organizations that as a consequence are able to influence the way our societies grow and develop. Power has not devolved from the center to the periphery. It has been taken by those new actors on the global scene that have been able to forge large coalitions of individuals across boundaries on specific issues, thus creating a critical mass that cannot be ignored. Dispersion of power is thus another element of our new paradigm.

The coming into being of these power centers was spontaneous and in some cases gradual, almost silent. It was not the result of elections or of a devolution of power, nor of any other kind of structured decisions taken by the actors of the old paradigm. The growth of these power centers is linked to their ability to galvanize a large group of people in different countries in the shaping of choices of a given society. They are by and large issue-driven, and issue-driven at the global level. They do not purport to offer a philosophy of life on every single aspect, but they claim to express the voice of human solidarity on an issue-by-issue basis. It is in a way ironic that having no popular mandate, and in some cases little accountability, they nevertheless project a voice.

The very contradiction of this point says much about the fluidity of power today. These new centers are powerful, and they can influence choices of entire societies, at times even of the global society. Some of these groups do, of course, fall within the trap of protectionist interests, thus becoming part of that dimension of exclusiveness that the dialogue would try to overcome. But in a more general way, they justify their actions on the basis of their claim for more democratization of the decision-making process and of safeguarding the interests of the entire planet. They project their own position as the antithesis of the elitism and exclusivism of powerful groups of governments, institutions or financial centers.

This kind of dispersion of power is, therefore, by itself a step towards the democratization of the decision-making process, for the more that traditional decision-makers will need to take into account other voices, the more the process of democratization will move forward. The new informal power centers still have a long way to go to live up to the requirements for accountability, transparency and legitimacy that are imposed on traditional institutions. However, there is little doubt that advocacy at the grassroots has become an effective tool to support various interests at the global or the local level.

The spreading of power in such an informal and unstoppable way seems to necessitate an approach based on dialogue. The different nature and structure of the power centers no longer allows them to meet and to communicate within the traditional institutions, and there is not yet a proper way, perhaps, to value and to weigh the role, the credibility and the power of these new actors. Unavoidably, a solution will have to be found as to how to structure the dialogue between these entities and the traditional institutional power centers. Clearly, these new power centers have come to the surface because they filled a vacuum; that vacuum was generated when many at the grassroots level felt that their institutional formal representations were insufficient or incomplete, unable or unwilling to hear or to process their voices. If the choice is between ignoring those voices or channeling them through a new kind of decision-making process, clearly the choice is simple. For the major powers choose to ignore the voice of the grassroots only at their peril.

What makes these new power centers so different in nature is their ability to bypass the borders that are the limits of power for the traditional structures. Unquestionably, national governments remain the power centers *par excellence* and still retain much of their ability to perform a role that nobody else can. At the same time, they may have to accept that it is a necessity to engage in dialogue with new players on the stage of the entire world whose strength may vary greatly according to the issue at stake.

The dispersion of power affords not only many more groups but also even individuals the opportunity to affect "the course of history." The ability to access knowledge, to communicate and to receive communications that has been for a long time the monopoly or quasi-monopoly of traditional power centers is now becoming more and more available to a larger set of individuals and groups outside the traditional structures. In some cases, of course, even the access to the use of force, which has been a predominant monopoly of the nation-state, is now available to nonofficial actors.

Access to knowledge and receiving and passing on communication is no longer mediated by the official and traditional powers. The nation-state still dispenses and provides security, but access to knowledge and communication is no longer mediated through the traditional structures. As access to knowledge and communication becomes more widely spread, power becomes more dispersed. Knowledge and communications provide the ability to influence, and influence is the first step to power. The power is accordingly more dispersed because the barriers and the borders to knowledge have been broken.

Political representation as we know it today was invented at a time when the mechanisms of communications were rather diffused and communication was brokered by the institutional power. In that environment, the mechanism of political representation was synonymous with indirect representation. That mechanism remains valid to this day, but it is being challenged by the search for more direct forms of representation, or even by self-representation.

The dispersion of power will sooner or later bring to the fore a more direct debate between representative democracy and direct democracy. Are today's parliaments tomorrow's mechanism for power representation? Not an easy answer, and that by itself perhaps underlines the change in paradigm. We are not offering an answer to what could replace representative democracy, and we are not advocating direct democracy as being a quick solution or even a realistic one. But it is a fact that the very institutions that embodied representative democracy are being challenged. Both nationally and internationally we are likely moving in the direction where our societies will have to tackle the mechanism of power representation and discover perhaps new forms for larger participation in the decision-making processes; and it will not just be a matter of numbers. The dispersion of power has already shown that even those who do not make decisions may influence them. They may also have the ability to provide checks and balances to the decision made, and eventually will demand participation in decision-making processes.

The very fact that some who exercise influence today are self-appointed is challenging the paradigm based on the election as a mechanism to delegate power. It seems that under the new paradigm, power can be had even without elections, and while that was true to some extent even in the past, it is truer today in a much wider sense. It is not only influence due to wealth, it is also influence due to beliefs, values and human solidarity.

The anomaly of the new actors on the international scene is not so much their diversity compared to the nation-state, but the nature of their "mandate." One could argue that some are self-appointed and there is no verification or control of their mandate. On the opposite side of the spectrum, it could be said that their mandate becomes legitimate through their staying power or their ability to remain active on the international stage. For their own effectiveness is to some extent a legitimization of their mandate. Clearly, there are no election processes for many of the groups that are now onstage. Yet, the real criteria for the new actors on the international scene is nothing less than credibility: credibility in the eyes of a number large enough to support them, to advocate for them and, in some way, to feel their voice spoken through them. Interestingly enough, and quickly enough, international public opinion and indeed nation-states seem to have accepted the newcomers; international intergovernmental institutions and intergovernmental bodies do make room for the new actors in different ways in their deliberation processes. At the other end of the spectrum, governments have to take into account the action of terrorist groups without debating their mandate too much. What has become clear is that the new actors have a variety of ways to be effective and to show their power. For many of them, one could argue that communication is a very important instrument of their effectiveness, and their power in communication is not just at the local level but also at the global level.

Dispersion of power means also requests or potential requests for more direct participation, and less mediation of power; there will be less need for a middle man but more need for new mechanisms to feed one's will and one's views directly into the decision-making process. To be sure, the role of the intermediary in the power structure has been challenged by other developments already. The growing role of the media and the wider access to information have already affected the role of elected representatives. Dialogue as a methodology becomes therefore more and more necessary. If we are moving toward a social structure with fewer intermediaries and more and more direct participants, some form of dialogue appears to be a wise methodology and a global ethic may become a common need.

The proliferation of new actors on the global scene, which has shattered the monopoly of the nation-state as the only player; the increasing role of the non-state actors—due to their credibility at times—and their access to information and communication; the "new meaning" of borders and divides that are less and less controllable by any authority; and, most of all, a widespread demand for dignity and justice—or at least the hope for justice—are likely to make the search for a new paradigm even more compelling. Perhaps the democratization of the international system was never planned to be this way. One could hardly envisage a search for a new order in the 1970s that would include private corporations, private individuals, linguistic communities or religious communities, identified as new possible players on the international stage. What has made it possible for this to happen was the breaking down of old barriers, be they technological, financial, political and, to some extent, even psychological, during the last twenty years. But perhaps most of all, what has made possible the proliferation of new actors on the international stage has been their ability to communicate and therefore to have an impact much beyond the confines of their location or origin.

Unavoidably, the next step will be the continuous challenge to traditional institutional frameworks by these new actors who are so at variance with the actors of the old paradigm. They will likely make dialogue more vibrant and more profound than it has ever been before among nation-states, as both partners and competitors. They will want to be featured more and more on the stage of the new global system that is being shaped.

### Stakeholding

The old paradigm of exclusion is based on the implicit or explicit acceptance of a "zero-sum game," that is, a situation where there is always a loser and a winner. It is also based on the strong need for an enemy. Both "exclusion" and "enemy" are not germane to a reality where power is dispersed. The old paradigm relies on the perception that there are losers and winners, in fact that to win, someone else must lose. It seems legitimate at this stage in the evolution of human society to ask the question: does the zero-sum game still apply?

The understanding of the entire planet as a unique eco-system, the realization of the borderless world of contagious diseases, the real-time communications that in many cases have overcome space, the incomparable ability for so many to hear so many others and, better yet, to communicate their own voices across so many divides and the overwhelming reality of economic globalization seem to make the point that there is a common world out there that we all share.

Those who hold dear in their hearts and minds the eco-system of the earth, which is one; those who hold dear the objectives of the free market, which they believe is one; and those who hold dear the dignity and human rights of their fellow human beings irrespective of their latitude or longitude on this planet have something in common. They all believe that we are part of the whole, of the world community that is interconnected and whose parts mutually affect each other. The greens, the global financiers and the human rights advocates perhaps unknowingly share a common vision: that the world is one for all, and we are all component parts of that entirety. In other words, each assumes that it has a stake in the world.

As the example of Thailand's economic crisis of 1997 illustrates, the time when major powers influenced the small powers without worrying about *vice versa* is long gone. In different ways, we are able to affect each other no matter what the geographical distance that separates us. The arrogance of ignorance may still be alive and well in the minds of some, but the belief of being untouchable by whatever happens many miles away has become an illusion. If nothing else, surely terrorism has driven home the point that we are no longer an island, and each of us can be affected by developments that we may have chosen to ignore.

The increased ability we all have to affect each other's lives, not only across distance but also beyond time, makes us accountable. Our children will inherit more than just our estates; they will also inherit the damage or the improvements we have made to world society in its physicality, its beliefs and dreams. This ability to affect future generations for better or, tragically, sometimes for worse surely is a powerful argument that proves not only the wholeness of the world in three physical dimensions but also the wholeness of the world in the fourth dimension, that of time.

The ability we possess to affect each other's lives in time and space as never before in history makes each of us in a way more deeply and more truly part of the whole. Accordingly, it makes us stakeholders of the entire world, in the sense that each of us has a global responsibility. With this reality, the very theory of winners and losers is starting to have less meaning.  If we are all stakeholders of the same unit, we may in fact find ourselves to be either jointly losers or jointly winners. It is an evolutionary process that has not happened in the past twenty-four hours, but clearly it already has begun to happen. The dynamic of dialogue may well increase not only the ability to affect each other but indeed also the knowledge that we are affecting each other. A whole ecosystem prospers when each part is allowed to perform the role that has been given to it in the cycle of perpetual life and death.

Stakeholding fundamentally questions the very concept of "us" and "them," leading to the discovery that our own good may also be—at the same time—the good of the other. The sense of being a stakeholder is therefore a fundamental ingredient of the new paradigm that we are trying to sketch. Paradoxically, the discovery of a stakeholding role in this world may come not as a result of our altruistic nature, but rather as a necessary requirement for a better life for each of us, and maybe even for our survival. Stakeholding is going to increase rather than decrease, if for no other reason than that the sheer number of inhabitants of this world requires each of us to better understand our role as a part of the whole.

The Universal Declaration of Human Rights in its first article states that "All human beings are born free and equal in dignity and rights." Acceptance of diversity and respect for others' dignity requires that parties have something at stake. If an individual shares an appreciation and respect for human dignity, he or she has an interest in other people's respecting his or her own dignity as well, and in their choosing to act in ways that do not affect other people's lives adversely. In other words, we are responsible for each other as stakeholders of the same enterprise. A successful world where human dignity prevails is one where we will really become in a global sense and in a specific sense each other's keepers, and where in fact we will be able to positively sustain each other's dignity in a very direct and practical way.

As stakeholders, we expect to act for the good of the whole because it makes sense, and we expect others to act the same way. The highest "stake" of the human stakeholding society would appear to be human dignity. While human dignity leads us to look at the individual in his and her uniqueness and "individuality," stakeholding leads us to think of the partnership in which we are linked and are thus part of society. The two may seem to be contradictory at first; but perhaps it is this duality that better explains the reality of social life and indeed its aspirations. The two sides of the same coin, the individual and society, are reflected in the concept of stakeholding and human dignity as the highest stake.

It would seem that the debate between those who attribute a higher significance to the individual and those who attribute a higher significance to community would find a reconciliation in the stakeholding mindset. For those who believe that individual rights should be held in higher respect than the rights of the community, stakeholding provides a sense of belonging to something larger than the individual, a sense of respect for something larger than the individual and a sense of understanding that there is a community to which every individual belongs. For those who highly value the rights of the community over those of the individual, stakeholding provides a sense of respect for each component of society, it provides a recognition that there are others beyond and above even our own community and it provides the sense of acceptance that damaging even one individual is in fact harmful to the entire community. Thus the concept of stakeholding would also be helpful to reconcile not just two schools of thought but two mentalities and two ways of looking at our common world.

The dispersion of power both directly and indirectly supports stakeholding. The new power centers, as we have mentioned, are driven by global issues, or at least issues that are wider than one single nation. The building of a new power center based on issues requires, therefore, a horizontal link of individuals across borders of different nations, individuals who thus share the same vision of the issue in question and thus have begun to practice their role as stakeholders in the community of human beings. Their actions are then based on the acceptance that we are all responsible, for example, for the degradation of the environment, no matter what our geographic location.

The new informal power centers are founded on the sense of stakeholding in a much larger entity than the one in which they immediately reside. The new informal power centers exist because they believe in responsibility vis à vis the entire planet, not just vis à vis one local authority. The dispersion of power also produces some kind of empowerment to so many more, and with that, a sense of ability to actually affect change. As a consequence, more people have come to have responsibility, as individuals or small groups, for issues that are so much larger. There may be, of course, confusion between having a vested interest in a larger issue or having a stake in it.

While a large number of individuals today feel themselves to be stakeholders in the destiny of the entire planet, a much larger number, unfortunately, have not yet had a chance to feel they have something at stake. A smaller, but powerful, number of individuals in ignorance and arrogance have clung to the anti-historic belief that they can save themselves even if the rest of the world collapses. The isolationists, the racists, the sexists, those who hate others because of diversity, may not be many in number, but they are surely dangerous, for their beliefs are blinded by their ignorance. There are those who still believe that physical distance will protect them, that they can remain uncontaminated by the reality of a world in which they do not believe and which they do not see as being interdependent. They are a mixed bunch, this group, because they include individuals with a high level of formal education as well as individuals with no learning at all. They are joined together by their fundamentalist belief in some kind of perverse sense of superiority passed on to them in some form or another. They may be poor in means, but they still carry an elitist mentality and a sense of contempt for everybody else. Can we ever truly become stakeholders if we equate diversity with enmity?

But for those who do not feel they have anything at stake because they are marginalized in one way or another, the way to feel a sense of belonging to a macro-entity may only come about through human solidarity. The sense of belonging is clearly an inherent element of stakeholding, but so is the sense of responsibility. The marginalized may not feel either. In this respect, globalization would actually fail if it could not reach an ever larger group of individuals. However, the real sense of stakeholding also implies the recognition of those who are marginalized, and a sense of responsibility to "cross the divide" in their direction.

Governments and institutions in the international system have devised programs to cross the divide and reach those less fortunate around the world. At the economic level, for instance, the concept of foreign aid as well as the policies developed by international organizations were aimed at the actors as we knew them in the past, namely, the governments. One economic instrument that has been developed over the last decade and a half, and which is at odds with the traditional institutional instruments, is the idea of microcredits and the ability, therefore, to make even single individuals in a very limited way have something at stake in a much larger system. The microcredit idea is not the result either of institutional policies or of the actors of yesteryear; it is in fact the product of the mind of one single individual and the hard work of many other individuals. The activities that are carried out by many NGOs at the very grassroots level, particularly in these areas, are slowly offering a stake in one's own empowerment to many individuals in many different countries. It seems to us to be the most successful example of creating stakeholders out of those who felt marginalized, and indeed were. The microcredit idea is quite remarkable also because it combines the sense of creating a stake with the sense of individual responsibility, thus creating a virtuous circle that changes not only economic conditions but also mindsets. The dispersion of power is another benefit of this development.

The question that has to be raised is whether there is stakeholding at the global level or whether stakeholding applies only to smaller groups. There can hardly be stakeholding at the global level if there is no global common denominator. Respect for human dignity surely is—we believe—an accepted common value. One could argue that the more one feels bound by defending human dignity, the more she or he proves that there is global stakeholding. Is this done only by heroes or exceptional individuals? Not really. The concept that we only save our own is disproved by the hundreds of thousands of people working across the divide for humanitarian and other reasons, who prove on a daily basis the human bond beyond the borders of any divide and irrespective of any divide. It is also disproved by the international solidarity shown by many governments in cases of natural disasters and other situations. Can we deny international human solidarity as a legitimately felt aspiration of many? If we cannot, then we have to concede that stakeholding at the global level is a possibility.

The ability of individuals, groups and states to affect one another makes them all stakeholders in global society and imposes upon them a global responsibility. This sense of being a stakeholder is a fundamental ingredient in the new paradigm.

### Individual Responsibility

Collective decision-making in some form or another has been the answer of societies to the whims of monarchs and tyrants. Over time, we have become accustomed to identifying institutions or collective bodies as decision-makers, not individuals. Both jurisprudence and political ideologies have gone a long way in making decision-making fairly anonymous, for good reason. The individuals who form part of those institutions, bodies and organs represented not themselves but other institutions, organizations and bodies. They were the voice of other collective nouns. But it was also convenient to hide the individuals behind the anonymity of those collective decisions. It was so convenient that unavoidably there were abuses. But perhaps a feature of the old paradigm of international relations was that collective decision-making almost automatically opened the door to the concept of collective responsibility. And collective responsibility easily became nobody's responsibility.

Over the last ten years, the question has been raised as to whether collective responsibility is the only form of responsibility in international affairs. The question is whether there is individual responsibility even in collective decisions. If not, would the individuals who participated in the decision-making feel the same level of commitment to carry out their decision as they would if they were individually responsible? Would their decisions be taken more lightly if only collective responsibility were at stake? Collective decision-making has been a considerable advancement of democratic decision-making since the overthrow of one-person rule. It is a great achievement of mankind to make decisions collectively by the elected representatives of the people. However, collective decision-making processes cannot cover up the responsibilities of individuals who participate in the decision-making. Each and every participant is, of course, aware that he or she is accountable to his or her constituencies.

The spectacle of an individual leader or soldier convicted of crimes against humanity and torture in a war crimes tribunal is a new sight in a world torn by violence against civilians in the 1990s. Is the establishment of the United Nations international war crimes tribunals a novelty in international society? For the first time in history, they are aimed at judging the behavior of the victors as much as that of the vanquished. In this sense they represent a qualitative change in international civil society. Implicitly, the tribunals have opened the door to questioning the concept of collective responsibility. It is a major development. Will it make each of us more conscious of our own burden as we act in the international arena and as members of institutions? Does this mean that institutions are not responsible but the individuals who act in the name of those institutions are first and foremost also accountable in person? There is no doubt that the Pandora's box has been opened. Are we on the way to reducing the cases when any individual, no matter what his or her title, can be considered beyond or above the law? Is it safe to say that when anybody violates the human dignity of another, there will be accountability?

Perhaps it is too easy to end the conversation by saying that the establishment of the war crimes tribunals has opened the doors, which until then had been completely shut. Perhaps the question of individual responsibility in international relations is also a consequence of the fact that the actors in the international scene are not only the nation-states but also small groups and individual persons whose credibility is sufficient for them to play a role. Perhaps we have gone full circle from the time societies took away the decision-making ability of one ruler, the king or queen, and handed it over to the collectivity, and began rightly to protect the individual from the decisions taken on behalf of the collectivity. Perhaps as in many other situations in human history, the abuse by some individuals of their position has broken the spell, and the war crimes tribunals were established. But perhaps we have gone even further than that. If individual responsibility is creeping up on the world of international affairs, it is also due to a larger sense of the common good and of common destiny for local society and society at large, and to a sense of the power of the individual. At some level, we are beginning to realize that in some instances, an individual's failure to act can be as damning as being actively involved in an atrocity. The inaction of the individual can be devastating. Many believe that the Holocaust could not have taken place if it were not for the willingness of individuals to passively accept what was being done to their neighbors. Many courageous people did take action and intervene, risking their own lives, but they were simply too few.

If one side of the coin is individual responsibility, the other side is that we are all stakeholders of our societies and indeed of the planet in which we live. This concept has now been accepted even more readily than that of individual responsibility in international affairs. In fact, it came onto the scene much earlier in time. This sense of planetary stakeholding was at the origin of NGO pressure on governments to eventually convene the Stockholm and Rio conferences on environment and sustainable development. They have opened a door that cannot be shut. That stakeholding carried with it a sense of solidarity across borders, the realization that what we do on one part of the planet will eventually affect others in another part. This contribution may well represent the best in international society today. It is a sense of solidarity, which contains also the unavoidable requirement of individual responsibility.

The paradigm engendered by dialogue is one where the sense of global solidarity and of individual responsibility will proceed hand in hand, for it is hard to commit oneself to anything at all if that commitment cannot be measured and tested in one's own life. The good news is that irrespective of what the laws of any country say, today scores of individuals have taken upon themselves the responsibility of being citizens of this planet, citizens of the world, caring individuals ready to contribute individually, to cross the divide, to take the personal decisions that together with millions of other decisions taken by other individuals will make a difference. The force and appeal and the impact of the "example" have been proven in history to be devastatingly effective. A single individual example can change the world. Moses, Confucius, Buddha, Jesus, Muhammad, Mahatma Gandhi, Martin Luther King, Jr., Mother Teresa and Nelson Mandela changed the way we view our responsibility towards our fellow human beings. It is the commitment of a few that has shaped and changed the world by inspiring so many. Some called them the apostles, others called them the elites, others called them the *avant garde* and still others called them "the flowers of the revolution." They were all using different names for the same handful of individuals who took responsibilities upon their own person and carried with their example the multitudes.

Can we say that individual responsibility had taken a leave of absence from international affairs? And that today more and more voices are calling for it to come back? In a real dialogue, one between individuals and institutions, between the powerless and the powerful, between the downtrodden and the super-organized powers that be, individual responsibility is perhaps another way to protect and to save the individuality of each of us, the originality of each of our thoughts, from the onslaught of hegemony and homogeneity of the majority or of the most powerful.

The responsibility of the individual is more necessary today, as the individual has more access to real-time information than ever. That access provides a new level of freedom, for it allows the individual to listen to others and to pass on his own views to others almost independently from institutions, structures and authority. The role played by information technology in the uprising in Palestine as well as in the Kosovo situation are only examples of the new access to others and to information that has become part of our reality. In a way, the individual is becoming more powerful and more sophisticated in every society, and the chance for any structure to deal with an entire population as a herd of sheep is less and less possible.

Individual accountability in international relations is coming of age slowly and with much opposition, but nevertheless it is growing. The financial crisis in East Asia in 1997 and 1998 had many negative consequences, but also some positive ones, including a consensus on the part of the intellectuals and thinkers in Asia that corruption and cronyism are to be countered and that East Asia could never build a world-class economy without embracing the international ethic of transparency, integrity and accountability. This is a very pervasive movement in Asia now, to the extent that during the rioting and demonstrations in Jakarta, the students were campaigning against "corruption, collusion and cronyism." This new ethic affects not just politicians but also the business community and citizens.

As power has become more dispersed and the number of actors on the international scene has increased, it would follow that responsibility in international affairs is not confined only to political leaders but applies also to corporate leaders, NGO leaders and individuals who have an influence in shaping the way society is going to be. As corporate leaders in particular have become more prominent and, in some cases, more powerful than some political leaders, they have taken on responsibility for issues beyond the profit-making activities of their respective corporations. They, like leaders of advocacy groups, represent the new unelected powers. In many ways, their power goes beyond voters; their influence certainly does.

Is individual responsibility in this case confined and determined exclusively by the writ of the law, that is, national laws? Does responsibility grow proportionately with the exercise of power? Does responsibility grow with power and *vice versa?* If so, does it mean that the most powerful are also the most responsible? Individual responsibility is slowly coming of age, as we said earlier, but most importantly the answers to the questions we have raised can only be found in the context of a new global ethic. The powerful country, the corporate leader, the politician and the media person are required to pay heed to a global ethic, as indeed they are unequivocally stakeholders of the entire planet.

### Issue-Driven Alignments

The old paradigm was one of ideologically strong alliances. Friends were friends on all issues, unquestionably and totally. Alliance was the name of the game because boundaries were rigid. Within each boundary, alliances had to be equally rigid. Crossing the divide was considered crossing into the enemy camp, no matter what the issue, no matter what the time. Typically, the old paradigm is well symbolized by the military alliances of yesteryear, where enemy and friend are as clearly defined as day and night, without twilight or sunset and sunrise. By contrast, today's world has allowed the creation of alignments driven by specific issues across formerly insurmountable divides. The alignments we see today not only are issue-driven but also are of a horizontal nature. Groups in different nations may link up with groups in other nations and pursue an objective, an interest or an aspiration that has little to do with the boundaries of yesteryear, and much more to do with the commonality of a world that is becoming, slowly but surely, more and more one.

Both institutional and noninstitutional actors are engaged in issue-based alignments rather than ideological alliances. Friendly governments may agree on some issues and disagree on others, thus creating alignments with the "enemy" of yesteryear on a specific issue. The AIDS epidemic has generated alignment between African countries and the West. The social, religious and political developments in Afghanistan have pulled together countries as varied as Iran, Russia, China, India and the United States. Carbon dioxide emissions are creating a common front among Europeans, Chinese, Indians, Iranians and South Americans. The power of the threat is forcing alignments without benefit of choice of allies. It seems as if different peoples and different countries are being pushed to work together against a common threat of great magnitude by the nature of the threat itself, rather than by their own choice.

Global threats may well have deprived many of the luxury of choosing their allies and forced them into alignments that are most notable for their diversity. The feature of these alignments is the common purpose of action on one particular front. Members of the same alignments join forces for one particular purpose, but they retain their diversity and their uniqueness in all other matters. In fact, to a large extent, they retain their disagreements.

One factor pushing issue-driven alignments is that power and influence are exercised sometimes in informal ways, by new groups and groupings that feel their allegiance not as much to the nation-state and the authority of the nation-state, but rather to the entire human race and even to the planet itself. Claiming their allegiance to a "higher authority" than the nation-state, they claim their role and their voice, not as a result of an election or a popular choice, but as the sum of individual choices. Alignment on issue becomes, therefore, more natural for those unstructured new centers of power that we tried to depict in the section on dispersion of power. For their point of reference is no longer borders, as it is for traditional power centers, but more fluid and undefined interests, aspirations and even human solidarity. Alignment on issue becomes, therefore, more germane to the unstructured power centers of a globalized world.

Alignments on issues are also being facilitated by access to knowledge across borders. We have discovered, for instance, that the same interest and the same aspiration can be shared by many people across many divides. Perhaps most importantly, issue-driven alignments to a certain degree have undermined the perception that diversity is a threat, for in many ways these alignments are fundamentally among individuals who share the same ideals or ideas but are quite different in terms of national, religious, ethnic or cultural backgrounds, race and gender. There is, of course, a negative evolution of issue-driven alignments, and that is the globalization of crime, terrorism, disease, money laundering and the like.

The concept of issue-driven alignments is a natural consequence of the other elements of the new paradigm. These unstructured alignments are easier in a society where individuals have taken on personal responsibility for their choices, and indeed for their actions. For they are struck by groups of individuals who have discovered common interests or common aspirations. Issue-based align-ments are also a natural consequence of the sense of stakeholding in the future of this entire planet, which many individuals feel, irrespective of their own national, religious or ethnic affiliation. Unquestionably, these alignments be-come easier in a society where empowerment, or the search for full empowerment, has opened the possibilities for equality, not only as an aspiration but as an achievable objective. Equal footing has empowered, in a way, even informal groups to search across borders for like-minded groups and individuals in different locations. Very logically, alignments based on issues are the evident consequence of a more dispersed power, for it is such a dispersion that has even created single-issue-driven power centers. Last but not least, the issue-based power center that forges issue-driven alignments has a different opinion of who is the enemy than the one traditionally portrayed for them by the traditional structures of power. The temporary oppo-nent may well be a corporation that pursues an industrial policy at odds with human solidarity as perceived by the alignment. On another occasion, the opponent may be a series of actors who do not respect the biodiversity of the planet; the nationality, religion or ethnicity of those oppo-nents is completely irrelevant for those who have joined forces in an issue-driven alignment.

In our view, the six elements of the new paradigm are al-ready detectable in some form or another in our present reality. In fact, they feed on each other, and they tend to strengthen each other in a quasi-systematic way. We be-lieve that the new paradigm will eventually become stronger because of this integration.

## C. Building Together

The last ten years have definitely put an end to the old paradigm, but they have also shown the absolute need for human dignity and hope for justice in front of incredible obstacles and overwhelming power. Equal footing, re-assessment of the concept of "enemy," dispersion of power, stakeholding, individual responsibility and issue-driven alignments are likely to emerge as more appropriate components of a paradigm that is responsive to the changing international scene.

Clearly dialogue in one form or another has been with us forever. The most useful dialogues are those among "enemies." As a famous prime minister once said, "You don't need to talk to a friend, you need to talk to an enemy." In noting the tendency to talk only to others who share one's viewpoint, John Stuart Mill advocated instead the need for communication across lines of difference.

> *If the opinion is right, people are deprived of the opportunity of exchanging error for truth; if wrong, they lose what is almost as great a benefit, the clearer perception and livelier impression of truth produced by its collision with error.*
>
> — *John Stuart Mill*, On Liberty, *1859*

In a more practical way, we are suggesting to go from a defensive dialogue, one where we seek to build protection from each other, to a dialogue where we seek common benefits and common interests until we reach a stakeholding status. There is no better way to reach that status than *to build something together across the divide.* In this way we will all have something at stake to jointly protect and nurture. A dialogue at the highest level, therefore, would be between two stakeholders—stakeholders not only in what they inherited but also in what they created together. The very success of dialogue will thereby be measured by what we build together across the divide. Building together is the ultimate response to the old motto that "might makes right." It is practically, conceptually and philosophically at the opposite side of the spectrum. Building together is the ultimate manifestation of the new paradigm.

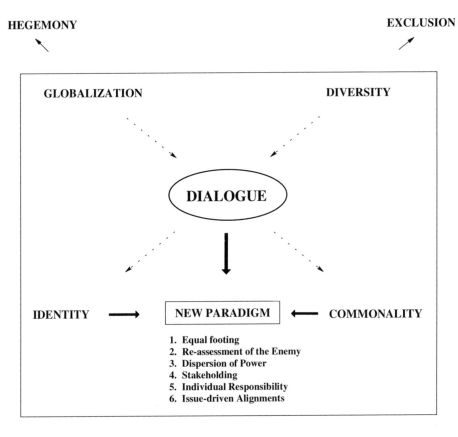

Figure 3

# CHAPTER 4

*About the United Nations*

*About the United Nations*

---

## A. A New Frontier for the United Nations?

Grandeur and misery both characterize the history of our globe. The history of humanity is great and sublime, but also infinitely cruel. From a historical perspective, the concrete ethical norms, values, insights and key concepts of religions and philosophies have been formed in a highly complicated social and dynamic process. Where basic human needs and concerns emerged, from the beginning of human history in every region of the world, there was pressure for regulation of human conduct: priorities, conventions, customs, commandments, instructions and laws—in short, particular ethical norms. For example, much that is proclaimed in the Bible as God's commandment is already found in the ancient Babylonian Code of Hammurabi from the eighteenth and seventeenth centuries BCE. Human beings have had to and still have to test ethical norms and ethical solutions in projections and models, often practicing them and proving them over generations. After periods of approval and acclimatization, such norms finally come to be recognized by a group, tribe, people or nation, but sometimes they are also diluted and replaced.

---

Are we perhaps living in such a time of change? Given the reality of our modern technological society, which is so multilayered, changeable, complex and often impenetrable, we need to use scientific methods to investigate, as far as possible without prejudice, the material laws and future possibilities of this society. Even today, the pre-scientific awareness of particular ethical norms, in so far as it still exists, retains basic significance for a high proportion of people. Happily, many people still "spontaneously" act correctly in particular situations without ever having read a treatise on moral philosophy or moral theology. Nevertheless, the exclusionary and hateful verdicts (for example, in connection with war, racism or the unequal situation of women) that have found their way into many religions and political regimes in the course of more recent history have been countered by development at the same time of ecological consciousness, feminist sensitivity, religious pluralism and a global ethic to one degree or another in different places. Has modern life become too complex for defining specific ethical norms? Has modern life fallen into a naïve blindness to reality that overlooks empirical data and insights confirmed by science?

A modern ethic depends on contact with the sciences: psychology and psychotherapy, sociology and social science, behavioral research, biology, cultural history, philosophy and anthropology. Responsible political or religious leaders and teachers need not show any anxiety in becoming involved in the human sciences, which offer a growing wealth of anthropological insights and information relevant to action, which can be used to facilitate equitable decisions. Even the physical sciences are, in the postmodern era, exploring the world of complexity, delving into the foundations of well-established theories in quantum mechanics and particle physics. New objects are emerging focusing on networks, dissipative and self-organizing phenomena. The impact of this upheaval is being felt throughout the world's intellectual society at large.

The central ethical questions are therefore raised all the more urgently. On what basic conditions can we survive as human beings on a habitable earth, and give humane form to our individual and social life? On what prerequisite can human civilization be rescued in the third millennium? What basic principles can be followed by the leading forces and institutions in politics, economics, science and religion? And on what basis can the individual achieve a happy and fulfilled existence?

Certainly all the states of the world have an economic and legal order, but this system cannot function without an ethical consensus, a civil ethic as the basis of democratic constitutions. Certainly the international community of states has also created transnational, transcultural and transreligious legal structures, without which international treaties would be sheer self-deception. But can we have a world order without a shared ethic for the whole of humankind?

### *Beyond Representative Democracy*

The demonstrations at the G-8 meetings in Genoa in July 2001, and the others that took place on the occasion of similar events, have taken many by surprise. To be sure, among the demonstrators, there were those whose behavior should not and will not be condoned, and whose voices should not be dignified, for clearly their objective was destruction for the sake of destruction. But many claimed to convey a message and a voice that they thought was not heard or given a chance. Whether rightly or wrongly, they represented an opinion and a group within societies that feel unrepresented. Are future meetings of the financial institutions and of the leaders of the industrialized countries going to be received by the same kind of reaction as we have seen since Seattle? Is this, in other words, a phenomenon of the world to come?

Leaders in general, and democratic leaders, in particular, claim to know the wishes of their population, indeed they feel they represent them well. They understandably have those feelings, for the system of democracy we have instituted in the majority of the countries of the world is a system where the will of the people is represented through the intermediary of their own institutions. For the last two centuries, representative democracy has been evolving through systems of checks and balances, with ever greater accountability and better communication between the population and the power intermediaries. Indirect democracy, to use another name for representative democracy, is not only the best we have been able to achieve, it is also the most efficient system we have been able to devise.

However, globalization may have unwittingly undermined that system of representation to an extent and in a way that we do not even know yet. The dispersion of power, the breaking down of the system of knowledge control, the "borderless society" that is emerging in different aspects of our lives, all have given direct voice to many more than ever before and provided the ability to communicate that voice to a wider audience than any single individual could dream of reaching in other ages. Simultaneously, this has created the ability to be in touch with like-minded individuals across borders, thus creating alignments of sorts that provide the critical mass for single-issue advocacy and, in the final analysis, create centers of influence.

If influence is, as we believe it is, the antechamber of power, the world we live in today is likely to become a world with many, many more power centers. Could it be that in Genoa we have seen various phenomena occurring: that representation in the structures of power may be less needed than it used to be; that power brokers are less and less sought after than in the past; and that indirect democracy is being challenged by nothing less than "its future"?

Intellectually, we can imagine direct democracy; theoretically we can envisage a system where each citizen has equal power and wants to exercise that power. In practice, we have come to equate direct democracy with anarchy and chaos. We do not know whether direct democracy will ever be possible; we do not know whether direct democracy will ever be good. More seriously, we do not have the answer to the challenge being raised by globalization to indirect democracy, which at the moment is the only system we can structure in a rather efficient way. The challenge will continue for the next few generations.

Has the United Nations a role to play in this unfolding epochal social adventure? Is the fact that the United Nations was built both for peoples and for governments in itself an inherent qualification to explore a new form of democracy? Are the attempts being made within the United Nations context to create a decision-making process where the nation-states and NGOs interact constructively the most immediate answer to that challenge? Is the very existence of a figure like the Secretary-General, neither government nor NGO, to be taken as an encouragement that the organization may have the imagination to be a bridge between the streets of Genoa and the palaces of Genoa?

It would be pretentious to suggest that we have an answer, because we do not, but we claim that the challenge exists. The provocative question is whether in ten or twenty years, our parliaments will be similar to the ones we have today, or completely different? It would seem logical to suggest that this is another reason why we have to develop our dialogue skills. The challenge to indirect democracy raised by globalization may require that we take dialogue to a level that we never considered before, a dialogue between those who ask for no intermediaries and the very institutions that have been created as intermediaries in the assembly line of power.

### New Constituencies

From a United Nations perspective, a successful process of globalization would produce a world where diversity lives in harmony with common values. In a larger perspective, this objective, if achieved, would also prove the value of the United Nations organization itself. But in the meantime, the institution will likely be pulled and pushed by the two opposing trends of our time: diversity and common values. At times, it will be asked to protect the uniqueness of diversity, and at other times it will be used to enlarge the common denominator of values. But it seems to us that if the organization and its leadership has set a vision for the future, whatever that vision is, it could hardly be achieved without appealing to a larger constituency than that which has traditionally been the United Nations community. While in many parts of the world, the peoples have been the beneficiary of a number of endeavors of the United Nations, the constituency has always been that of the membership, namely, the member states, and for good reasons. While that will continue to be the case, it is the support, the advocacy and the passion of other constituencies, unofficial constituencies, unstructured ones, which will in the end determine whether the United Nations can still be ahead of the pack of societal evolution. The existence of such constituencies, and the possibility of alignments in support of the United Nations across borders from civil society, will unavoidably enhance the credibility of the institution's activities and objectives.

To galvanize new constituencies, we may not need further restructuring, the intricacies of which may appeal to the staff of legislators and bureaucrats but hardly to the imaginations and minds of those who suffer or hope across the divides. To the new constituencies, which may vary from the media community, to the private sector, to the underprivileged and those without hope, to the oppressed and the victims, the United Nations will mean something if it is able to convey a message that no other institutional bureaucracy is able to provide, that no other leadership is able to communicate, and that no other politician has the courage even to imagine. In practical terms, there may be no shortcut in the future of the United Nations, only a charismatic leadership able to speak the language of reconciliation and truth, of personal responsibility and personal sacrifice and of examples over speeches.

These new constituencies may include what some would call a "public intellectual," a man or woman who is "culturally sensitive, politically concerned and socially engaged." This figure of the individual exists today in many places, from NGOs, to academia, to governmental institutions, to international organizations. It remains a fact that the United Nations has done much to contribute to the strengthening of the "public intellectual." It is this kind of individual who may reflect, better than most, the new paradigm that we described earlier. It is this individual who probably has internalized the sense of human equality, the uneasiness with the concept of enemy, the appreciation for the different forms of power in today's world, the sense of belonging to the same planet and the same human family, the acceptance of accountability and responsibility to each other and the understanding that he or she can share aspirations and values with many across borders.

Certain communities in particular may need to be brought into the workings of the United Nations in one way or another. Is it not logical to suggest that at a time of rapid technological evolution, at a time of biotechnology and genetic engineering, scientists might be brought to the front row of the work in the world body and contribute to the policy debates? This is even more fitting, perhaps, since the scientific community may have been the first to be globalized by necessity, much before the last decade began. Is a council of scientists, perhaps in an advisory role to the Secretary-General, a possibility in the near future? Much has been done to bring the contribution of religious leaders over the last several years into the work of the United Nations. Would it be useful for the organization to look at the future challenges and opportunities offered by science at its cutting edge, particularly in the fields of biotechnology, bioengineering and information technology? Is a "Security Council of Scientists" too far-reaching an idea?

Of course, civil society and private companies, academic institutions and media, while representing an important part of society, to a large degree are self-appointed and vary in their accountability to the population at large. The institutions of the nation-state remain at a different level exactly because, to a large extent, they are the expression of an electoral process; therefore they are "legitimate" in that sense, and they are accountable in a very specific way to the population they represent. The inclusion, therefore, of new constituencies may require a distinction between the roles of the nation-states and civil society, which remains to this day very unclear. The move to demand more accountability from our elected officials has not been mirrored by a similar move to demand more accountability from the new constituencies, which will be necessary if they become part of global governance. Is this leading towards a "General Assembly of Civil Society" within the walls of the United Nations, and if so, is a charter of rights and duties needed for those who then become part of this new structure?

## A Coalition of Institutions and Civil Society

The United Nations, like any other institution, has been affected by globalization. It may yet be premature to say what will be the result, but the wind that is blowing through "the house of glass" will have an impact on the way the organization is perceived and the way in which the organization will function. The institution, which is first and foremost one of nation-states, finds itself in the middle of a reality where so many new actors have increasing influence and a voice. Understandably, and correctly, the role of the nation-state remains central. But the voice of many individuals is also heard. Globalization, in other words, has brought to the forefront another duality that already existed within the institution, indeed within its own charter, namely, that between peoples and governments. In this context, the organization has been playing a positive role, so as to avoid this duality's being transformed into a confrontation, and instead to produce an even more effective decision-making process. It may have been one of the less appreciated and unconscious roles that the United Nations has played over the last ten or fifteen years.

Only a decade ago, the idea that the United Nations organization could have had as an interlocutor anything other than a government was considered blasphemy. But over the last few years, negotiations have been conducted, agreements have been reached, humanitarian cases have been resolved that required the participation of military groups, political organizations and even individuals, none of whom had the status or, in many cases, the legitimacy of a government. The fact that this process has taken place without impinging on the legal position of the nation-state has been nothing short of a success. Within the framework of the organization, in a way, the "peoples" of the United Nations and the "governments" of the United Nations have more often than not found a sort of reconciliation and, on many occasions, a real constructive cooperation. What seems to be emerging is an organization that has offered the previously unknown possibility of looking at the peoples and their governments in the international context in a cooperative manner, not in a confrontational one.

A major role in this process of forging the coalition may well be played in the future by the United Nations Secretary-General, a figure who may also be responsible for many of the United Nations' successes and the hope for more yet to come in a changing international world. Not a government, and not an individual; deprived of the traditional tools of state, namely, money and weapons; yet the Secretary-General is potentially "credible" in the very arena where power and might have been kings. Accordingly, it may be reasonable to suggest that the abnormality of the office called "the Secretary-General"—in between, so to say, a traditional institution, governments and a nongovernmental institution—may offer a better chance to deal with an international reality populated by different kinds of actors. Neither a government nor an NGO, the office of the Secretary-General is unique. It is no surprise, therefore, that in recent years the Secretary-General has been looking at other constituencies in the world at large beyond governments, and has done so reading, quite correctly, the changing reality: one where grassroots voices do not always need an intermediary to be heard. Dialogue becomes for the Secretary-General, therefore, the indispensable channel through which he or she can test his or her credibility, the strongest card that he or she can play. Of course, one would have to give a different meaning to the word "power" if attributed to a Secretary-General of the United Nations: hardly power in the sense of "might makes right"; surely power based on morality; perhaps power as credibility, no matter what the cost.

It may be easy to describe the institutions, both at the level of nation-states and at the international level, as being the "establishment" of this world, and civil society, on the other side, as being the non-establishment. The fact is that pitting institutions against civil society and *vice versa* is not necessarily a practical description of reality. Individually, we may belong both to the institution and to civil society at the same time. We may be leaders and followers on different topics; we may be both expert and ignorant. In a way, we have gone from a time when institutions were created first—and, accordingly, were supposed to represent and be the intermediary for the entire society—to times when institutions were seen as separate and apart from those whom they claimed to represent. Both views may be incorrect. There are many who still feel well represented by the institutions that exist, but many do not. Having recognized the two different dimensions of the lives of individuals within society, the institutional and the more informal, it would appear that only a coalition between the two would be able to respond to the challenges we face today. Is a coalition between civil society and institutions possible? It would appear that the very division between institutions and civil society has taken the discourse to a different level of freedom. Yes, there is more in society than the institutions; and yes, there is more in society than the individual. We accept that much already; we even accept that institutions may not provide the solutions to every problem and the answer to every question. But civil society has made the raising of questions its priority, and institutions have made answering those questions their priority.

What we have not yet put into practice is an ethic that needs to be really global, drawn from a coalition of civil society and institutions. A global ethic that is acceptable and accepted, implemented and lived, would have to be born out of such a coalition. There is no set manner in which a covenant between the two can be established. There are no conference halls in which we can fit the institutions and civil society in their entireties, but there are surely common values, as we have already seen, and there are also common beliefs that continue to emerge in this one planet in which we increasingly live together in real time. We are developing a global ethic as we develop this coalition between institutions and civil society, first and foremost through our common response to the unavoidable common threats and global problems before us. Because what happens in one part of the world is not only known in another but also affects so many and so far away, we have become more sensitive to great human tragedies, man-made or natural disasters.

These tragedies, be they the manifestation of the power of nature or the manifestation of the cruelty and perversity of the human mind, as in terrorist attacks, have produced a response from both civil society and institutions based on the same pillars of a global ethic: the longing and striving for peace, the longing and striving for justice, the longing and striving for truth and the longing and striving for partnership. It is sad if a coalition, as we have been mentioning, could emerge only as a reaction to negative developments, at least at first. But it is a fact that it is in the face of adversity that the core of a global ethic emerges in its most magnificent way. That core is *human solidarity,* and its ethical conceptualization is the *Golden Rule*, in its two different facets: not to do unto others what we do not want done unto us; and to care for others as we would like others to care for us. Perhaps these pillars of global solidarity have been weakened for too long by too many "ifs and buts." It would seem that as we become closer to each other, as we are able to affect each other more, the "ifs and buts" may fall by the sidelines, and perhaps our human bonds may eventually be strengthened.

In a way, the United Nations system offers a framework where one day the great coalition between civil society and institutions will be forged. Here again, it will not be a coalition of winners and losers, but it will be one that will succeed only if everyone wins. After all, institutions will survive only if they can respond to the questions raised by civil society in a satisfactory way, and civil society will take the lead only if it represents common beliefs, values and aspirations in respect, not fear, of the diversity we all so dearly cherish. To those who preach philosophy, ideology and sets of beliefs based on the unavoidability of conflict, confrontation and antagonism on the one hand, and bigotry, prejudice and exclusion on the other, we envisage instead a possibility of unity, of coalitions, of common values and of a global ethic.

The tragedy of September 11, 2001, was committed by people who perceive diversity as a threat, by people who needed to hate in order to be, a perversity beyond hope. Those who launched those attacks surely would like to see the theory of clash of civilizations fulfilled. It would be their ultimate success. We feel duty-bound today, therefore, to raise the banner of Dialogue among Civilizations higher than ever, to affirm the commonality of the human species louder than ever and to proclaim that for the few who kill their neighbors, many more know in their hearts that we are each other's keepers.

## B. From the United Nations to a Global Ethic

A universal institution is, by definition, duty-bound to take into account the global dimension and the diversity of each component. To be sure, the most immediate and practical reason for the establishment of the United Nations was the need to devise an institution that would prevent a third world war. In a way, a system of power grounded in reality was put into place with very practical objectives. The brutality of World War II surely required that any new system be anchored in the reality of power. Indeed, the new institution had to respond to the need for stability and predictability of behavior, both of which are based on power and respect for power. It was not surprising, therefore, that it was built on the core alliance of the victors. It had to be reassuring, and in a way it was. Yet there was more to it.

On the face of it, globalization and diversity do find a natural meeting place in this human enterprise that consciously developed around the pillar of dialogue. The very idea was to meet on a level of common values, to respect each other's sovereign dignity and to build together solutions based on the notion that might does not make right. Over the years, the institution has evoked different images in the minds of many, envisioned by some as a panacea to human folly, despised by others as a Trojan horse of the enemy and perceived by fewer still as a first endeavor to realize a dream yet unfulfilled after thousands of years of human history.

In the context of our reflection, perhaps the most relevant question about the past of the United Nations is not to count how many solutions to conflicts it has contributed, how many children's lives it has improved, how many refugees it has sheltered, or how many lives it has saved. Perhaps the question is whether the institution has been able to generate a new mindset among those who have come to work with it, work in it or benefit from it over the last sixty-some years.

Was it possible for an institution that had so many roots in the past and an idealistic vision of the future to generate its own mindset over the years that could really and profoundly transcend the mindset of each? When it was set up, the United Nations swung between two quite different images: the United Nations of the peoples and the United Nations of the governments. It was probably correct to create this conceptual tension between the peoples and the governments, for it is a tension that legitimate governments do not fear; and those that do may reveal much about their legitimacy, or lack thereof. Sixty years ago, the nation-state was not yet at the peak of its power. There is quasi-unanimity today that the nation-state has now peaked. It will hardly remain the same after the globalization phenomenon has completed its cycle, which may, of course, take a number of generations.

The office of the Secretary-General of the United Nations is not a job; it is a mission. It is not a coincidence that those who were best at it were those who felt it in that way.

Throughout the many restructurings of the organization, and throughout the reforms and the various financial crises that also occurred with regularity, the world organization seems to have adapted rather well to the changing needs of member states. To a nonpolitical observer, it would appear as if the member states were obsessed with controlling the organization, which, by their own definition, at various times was weak, irrelevant or ineffective. The fact was that the organization was always an anomaly to the nation-state, and yet it was more than just an intergovernmental body. That, perhaps, was the very essence of the mixed feelings that the United Nations generated in the capitals of the member states. Now, of course, the real challenge for the organization and its member states is that power has been dispersed much beyond the boundaries of traditional institutions, and the players on the scene are not always elected, accountable or even identifiable.

It is ironic that the very institution of the Secretary-General continues to provoke so many political emotions. After all, that office can neither levy taxes nor move military divisions. Could it be that the very fact that it has no money and no weapons, yet it still has an impact on various portions of the world, is a sign of another success of this incredible human endeavor: to have power without the main ingredients of it? The person in that position will find himself or herself in good company in the years to come, for power without money or weapons has become a more familiar feature. In fact, it seems that the strength of anybody occupying that position resides in ideas, principles and communication.

Most of all, the figure of the Secretary-General has been able to adapt to the changing international environment. This flexibility has made it possible for the person who occupies that position to become more useful to the international community and to the member states in particular at different times. Very rightly, the role of that anomalous position seems to have been most successful when it has helped the member states to do what they would not or could not do. So, for instance, it was through the Secretary-General that member states were able to resolve, in the early nineties, the problem of civilian hostages detained in Lebanon; it was through the Secretary-General that communications between new and old enemies could be transmitted; and it was through the Secretary-General that nonmember states, in fact, relevant actors that were not states at all, were able to have their voices heard and, in some cases, constructively engage with governments.

In practical terms, the most successful Secretaries-General were those who found their role to be complementary to that of the member states and also of the Security Council, and not in competition with them. Perhaps historically, the clearest case in this regard was the role the Security Council and the Secretary-General performed in their handling of the Iran-Iraq war, and their successful achievement of a cease-fire in 1988. The flexibility of the Secretary-General has increased over the years to include the ability to become a useful interlocutor with civil society, the private sector, religious organizations and advocacy groups, all of whom have acquired a role in the shaping of our new societies. So the second success of this human endeavor may have been the creation of a significant international figure, even one without the traditional attributes of power.

The ability to generate consensus and to create common values is another undervalued contribution made by the United Nations to the human family. This is true even to the extent of harmonization of laws while respecting diversity and seeking the cooperation of the major legal systems of the world in identifying common principles. The United Nations has become the place for drafting new principles of international conduct, recognizing customary law and crystallizing custom into new law codified in treaties.

The organization has thus become the site for progressive development of international law. Commercial arbitration rules have developed through the United Nations machinery and are extensively used; basic sales of goods in international business transactions are governed by a convention originated within the United Nations framework. It is a body of common rules directly affecting the lives of individuals and not only the behavior of governments. Environmental concerns, human rights and protection of the weak, be they children or others, have been made to leapfrog from local issues to global issues as United Nations conferences and conventions on these matters became a reality. Concerns have become global well before becoming matters of binding international law.

It is perhaps interesting to remember here that one of the "battles" fought within and around the United Nations was over the concept of the international civil servant. Although it was portrayed almost as an East-West confrontation, we all know that East, West and South were almost all on the same side of the barricade when it came to this issue. The very concept of the international civil servant was attacked politically, ideologically, administratively and otherwise at all levels. There was a reason for this, but the very battle proves how the institution of the United Nations as a human endeavor contains a power that all traditional institutions feared. It was as if the very concept of *"international civil servant"* would have undermined the concept of *"nation-state."* How could one be a servant of the international community if the highest authority was the nation-state? How could one give allegiance to an institution that was not the nation-state? It is easy to understand how the right and the left of yesteryear found common ground on this question. It is easy to see how both sides of the political spectrum found new allies in those new countries that were just emerging onto the scene, and wanted first and foremost to establish their institutional existence. They may not have belonged either to the East or to the West, but they surely did not feel they could afford to support allegiances that were different from their own.

The battle over the concept of the international civil servant was an undeclared battle that ran across the entire history of the United Nations. One can claim it was undeclared, because any open declaration would have revealed the strange bedfellows (democracies and dictatorships) that lay on one side of the fence, and the very few indeed who had the courage to be on the other side. In a way, it is easier to talk about this today because the entire globalization phenomenon is transforming not only the nation-state but also the United Nations, and we may end up with international civil servants who exist not only within the boundaries of the world bodies but also outside them in academia, trade and business, science and NGOs.

Honor should be paid to those first international civil servants who weathered all kinds of attacks—intellectual, political, psychological and more—in an international environment where allegiance beyond the nation-state was, to say the least, poorly understood. In many legal systems of the world, the figure of the international civil servant did not even exist. In fact, in some systems it still does not. It was, of course, understandable, for giving a role to the concept of the international civil servant was misunderstood by some as tantamount to undermining, in a small way, the sovereignty of the nation-state. And so there were those who accused the international civil servants of representing the identities of the enemy, and there were others who simply disregarded them, for they did not fit into the narrow framework of being this or that nationality.

But despite it all, despite the Cold War, despite a North-South divide, despite the one-superpower era, there were many who actually developed a United Nations frame of mind. It was not uncommon to be asked—and be unable to answer as a United Nations civil servant—the question: "Why would you risk your life for somebody who is not a member of your family, or of your tribe, or of your nation?" It was not a lack of intellectual ability; it was rather the proof that the United Nations enterprise had been able to shape the mindset of some. It was not an inability to answer, but rather the inability to understand the meaning of that question. The new mindset created the feeling that we are all stakeholders of the human family and each other's keepers. Even though many would have ridiculed such a mentality, for a few others discovering or feeling allegiance and duty to each human being, irrespective of nationality, race, creed and gender, was probably the greatest test of humanity, and proof that the United Nations organization had been more successful than many would have thought.

Nevertheless, on a more sober note, the last decades have witnessed new attempts at undermining the concept of the international civil service, in deeds if not in words. The financial limitations of the organization, at the same time as new tasks were assigned to it, brought about a large number of officials "seconded" from their governments. Over time, the very structure of the career civil service has been attacked, and what appear to be technical modifications to the career structure have in fact introduced a sense of insecurity on one hand and, more profoundly, may have undermined its very meaning. On top of reliance on secondments from governments, the institution has seen limitations put on "career contracts," both of which in fact undermine allegiance to the organization. Nevertheless, irrespective of the contractual relationship between international civil servants and the organization, there will always be a number of them who will retain their allegiance to the world body, whereas a number of others will "play it safe" and keep their allegiance to the governmental institutions to which they will likely return. The fact is that the figure of the individual who feels his or her belonging to the world community and perceives the sense of human solidarity has developed both within and without the structure of the world organization.

The undiscovered potential of the organization lies in the large number of individuals who possess those qualities and who still work across the world in the name of the organization. They provide those who benefit from their actions in the small villages, in the faraway valleys and in the impenetrable jungles the only available image of the United Nations. It is this image of the United Nations that has very likely kept it still credible in the eyes of those who cannot afford the luxury of hiding the truth from themselves. It has been too easily forgotten that the organization has been successful, where it has succeeded, also because of the passion, the altruism and the ideals of the individuals working for a United Nations program, peacekeeping operation, specialized agency or refugee assistance program. These international civil servants have maintained the sense of credibility in the institution and the hope for what it can do. Beyond the papers, the conferences, the resolutions and the many speeches, it is those men and women, unknown to most, but very well known to those who benefit from their work, who deserve to be brought to the forefront of the organization. Furthermore, they deserve to be protected from the cheap, at times unjustified and often wrong attacks of political lobbyists from faraway places whose ignorance is probably their only excuse.

It will be said that idealistic international civil servants are few and that many are not so dedicated, and it may well be so. After all, the apostles, the vanguard, the elites, indeed the heroes throughout time have never been the majority, and yet they have been able to make, shape and write the history we have all inherited. The Dialogue among Civilizations is not an instrument that will lend itself to major restructuring of the United Nations organization. Dialogue is an instrument that may help those unsung heroes of the institution, together with those outside of it who are equally brave, succeed in changing a mindset from one of war to one of hope and reconciliation.

In a way, the greatest defeat for the organization may have been the inability to communicate the significance of its achievements to public opinion at large. The ability to create an international civil service that was able to withstand decades of misunderstanding and attacks; a role for the Secretary-General that could be useful to the member states and to individuals without being a threat to their own power; and the United Nations as a place where international law is created and implemented were all never really appreciated by a larger audience.

It is very difficult for those who have not experienced the mindset of the international civil servant at its best to appreciate what it really means, for it is like trying to see a picture of an object that you do not know exists. As for the Secretary-General, too many bureaucrats have looked at the role through the eyes of a contender, a competitor and, most of all, a player in a "zero-sum game" with the member states. The bureaucratic mentality of a national civil servant who looks at anything and anybody outside the nation-state as a potential enemy, or at least as a competitor, could not be overcome in sixty short years. As for the role of the United Nations in the creation and enforcement of new international law, too many nation-states fall back on claims of sovereignty, sometimes only at selective moments to further certain national policies, rather than embracing an international legal system that may actually benefit more of their citizens through compliance with global norms.

For whatever reason, the three concepts of the true international civil servant; of a Secretary-General who could not possibly ever be a competitor with governments; and a locus of international law creation, codification and compliance may have been concepts ahead of their time. However, today globalization may force all of us, the nation-states and the world organization, to change yet again, for as we have seen from Seattle to Prague, from Stockholm to Genoa, there is something more out there beyond intergovernmental institutions and nation-states. It is a sign of our times that only recently, a call for reform of the World Bank and the International Monetary Fund has been made in these terms:

> *A new Bretton Woods . . . would include representatives of the developing world as well as of the developed world; it would also include representatives of the non-governmental organizations and private sector leaders.*
>
> — *Felix Rohatyn, Former United States Ambassador to France,* Financial Times, *August 20, 2001*

The United Nations has already learned how to deal with some nonstate entities over the last decade, proving that the institution has flexibility and imagination. More may be needed to bring the NGOs and the private sector into the collective decision-making process. There is no road map for that. It will be nothing less than a first attempt to marry indirect democracy with direct democracy.

### Participation and Legitimacy

The very creation of the United Nations organization was a significant step in the establishment of the new international order that emerged from World War II. The United Nations was to reflect the common values of its members, the victorious allies; to demonstrate its universal appeal;

and, most of all, to represent the incarnation of international legality. The idea was very clear: no more right through might, but rather right through a system of rules equally accepted by all.

The equality of the members was represented by the rule of one country, one vote, thus embodying the simplest aspirations for justice, equity and fairness that could hardly be denied, at least on a theoretical level. In this context, perhaps, the General Assembly embodied an idealism that went beyond its time. Of course, the Security Council, by contrast, introduced a level of realism that was so characteristic of previous centuries. It represented the concept of a *directoire* of major powers, where special privilege carried with it a special responsibility. Typically, the Security Council and the General Assembly, the member states and the Secretary-General, the use of force in self-defense, and the desire to resolve conflicts by peaceful means, are but some examples of the dichotomy of the structure, a dichotomy that can simply be defined as one between reality and aspirations. The organization appeared to be well rooted in the reality of power while still aspiring to a higher level of fairness than was possible at any given time. One could say it was an organization well rooted in the past, but with a vision for the future.

The organization as such still has plenty to offer to its members, who are and remain, of course, the nation-states. It may be that we have not yet fully exploited the potentiality of this structure. To those who say that the United Nations is nothing more than the sum of its members, we beg to differ. Within the framework of the United Nations, we would like to submit that a global social contract is being consummated. This global social contract is based on the need for legitimacy by some, and the request for participation in the decision-making process by others. Both sides may refuse to grant what they possess, but both sides in part do possess one of the two currencies: either the ability to grant legitimacy or the ability to grant participation in the decision-making process.

The organization offers, as no other, a platform through which legitimacy may be secured. It does so because of the universality that is one of the characteristics of the United Nations. The same universality affords to all the possibility of being part of—though in different degrees—the collective decision-making process. Over the last ten years, we have witnessed the fact that the major powers do not go to the United Nations to receive financial or military support but rather to receive legitimacy for the course of action they plan to take, or in some cases that they have already taken. It is not an absolute necessity to receive that kind of legitimacy, but even the most reluctant isolationist will concur that, if given the choice, legitimacy through the United Nations is by far preferable to legitimacy through any less international body.

The problem, of course, comes when the price for this legitimacy has to be paid. That price is the participation in the collective decision-making that leads to an action. The level of participation may vary, but every successful, legitimate international action has gone through such a process. So the questioning of the organization may be less a question of structure and more a question of understanding how to consummate a contract between those who seek legitimacy for their actions and those who are prepared to grant it in exchange for some degree of participation in the decision-making process. This can happen both through a very formal process and through an informal one.

In reality, legitimacy and participation can only be exchanged through a system of communication, indeed a dialogue that is based on a sense of respect for the dignity and pride of each of the actors involved in the contract. In the context of this contract, each player has something to offer because, in a universal structure, everybody can contribute and can grant at least part of legitimacy. At its minimum level, a deal between legitimacy and participation requires communication between the two sides. This consultation itself may be a basic way of being involved in the decision-making process.

The recognition that this global social contract can be consummated within the framework of the United Nations may offer both the major and the smaller powers within the world body a redefinition of their relationship, beyond one based exclusively on power. At different times, suggestions for policies or solutions for crises may come from different countries. This may be due to different interests in different topics, or simply due to different priorities. For all those who at a given time suggest policies or solutions, there are others who may simply be interested just in being involved in the decision-making, rather than being the initiator of those policies or those solutions. At other times, their positions may be reversed. It would appear, therefore, appropriate that those who propose ideas and solutions seek legitimacy for their actions. It would accordingly stand to reason that, in a reality of increasing interdependence, others may wish to feel themselves to be coparticipants, in some form, of the collective decision.

Decision-making processes as such may still remain the exercise of a few, but influencing those processes has become easier today than ten years ago. Whether those who seek legitimacy for their decisions are prepared to offer participation in those processes or not, they are going to be influenced by others more than ever before. Influence may be indirect, informal and unstructured, but the dispersion of power as brought about by globalization is creating opportunities to affect decision-making processes. The United Nations framework simply offers an organized way through which this could happen.

Some of the agreements reached in the last ten years aimed at solving conflicts have been characterized by a high level of compromise, a compromise that some would say has sacrificed justice in favor of "peace." Those agreements, from the Balkans to the Middle East, could only have been reached at that moment in time, in the mid-nineties, when the ability to influence those who possessed might was weaker than it is today. It is very questionable whether in 2002 one could repeat what was achieved then with regard to "peace agreements"; chances are that we have gone beyond that. No wonder that those kinds of agreements that were not quickly implemented probably never will be. The request for participation, or at least the ability to influence the traditional power holders, is growing by the day.

Could one have peace without justice? Ten years ago and earlier, the common wisdom would have said that justice was not so easy to obtain, but that peace in the sense of stability was worthwhile securing. The last few years may have changed that perception. There may still be inequality in power and in might, but the kind of politics of power that leads to compromises of dubious ethics are more difficult to achieve. We may be entering an era where many would recognize and accept that justice is not always possible, but they may insist that a hope for justice should be there if peace is to be achieved. The dispersion of power and the limits to power of any given government have emboldened some to pursue objectives that may have appeared impossible only a decade ago.

During the Cold War, international solutions as a result of compromise were the order of the day. The compromise in the nineties was due in large part to the reality of the one-superpower system, the shock of which seems to have been digested. The myth of the invincibility of anyone may have come to an end. The economic slowdown starting in early 2000 in the three Northern trading blocs simultaneously, which is perhaps more worrisome than many would like to admit, is surely placing in a different perspective the myth of a victorious civilization and the illusion of the theory of the end of economic cycles. Nothing, of course, represents more dramatically the end of that "myth of invincibility" than the events of September 11, 2001, in New York and Washington, DC. History has not ended, but what seemed unavoidable yesterday may not be so any longer. We may even see the review of isolationist tendencies. The global social contract between legitimacy and participation not only may be possible in its true form but also may become desirable to many within the context of the United Nations. It may represent the last defense of the besieged nation-state: a contract that would strengthen the solidarity among the nation-states, if not among peoples. After all, the concern of many these days is that individual nation-states behave as if others did not exist, as if they were not part of a system with a body of rules. In other words, this syndrome of being "above the law" or "outside the law" may well be considered to be the greatest challenge.

In this respect one could argue that if the United Nations is the locus where a global social contract between legitimacy and participation is struck, it may yet become more effective. The need for such a contract will become increasingly self-evident, as power alone will not deliver peace any longer. In fact, in the limited constraints of the United Nations organization, the nation-state may still find a more comfortable environment for its decision-making process than in the "real world," where new, unelected, unaccountable and unstructured actors have already made themselves known through their ability to influence the decision-making processes on a global scale. In the end, at least for a number of years to come, the nation-states may find it convenient to come to an understanding within the confines of a structure like the United Nations that is monopolized by them.

To sum up, we can look at the world body as a place where "participation" and "legitimacy" are the two assets to be exchanged. In our view, dialogue that goes beyond words means an acceptance of the idea that those who seek legitimacy for their actions are prepared to offer participation in the decision-making process; and those who wish to participate in the decision-making process are ready to offer their legitimacy.

## Credibility

The universality of the United Nations organization and the diversity of its membership are at the basis of the tension between common values and identity. Some would look at common values and identity as incompatible with each other; others would simply see them as in a continuous struggle. The organization has suffered in its functioning because of these different perceptions of what seems to be a simple fact of life. To oppose common values in order to protect one's own identity is quite a defensive approach, one that reveals a sense of insecurity in that identity. The originality of one's own identity does not shine in isolation. It does so when one is engaged with others. The acceptance of common values does not diminish one's own identity, but we believe that identity can stand in an environment where common values exist. By the same token, just as isolationism cannot be a good test of one's own ability and qualities, for there is nobody to measure those qualities and abilities against, identity can better be appreciated in a context of common values.

The members who joined the organization start from a common denominator that is as basic as the Charter of the United Nations and as wide as the number of covenants and conventions that the majority of member states have undertaken since its founding. The strength of the United Nations rests on the very fact that it is not a super-governmental organization, and it is not trying to become a government of the world.

Throughout its life, the organization has been sensitive to, and resentful of, power; hopeful that international law will apply equally to all, yet occasionally engaged in double standards. The Cold War climate is, of course, primarily responsible for this kind of attitude. But the Cold War is also the genesis of another image with which the organization has fed itself for too long: "impartiality." Devised as an unconscious attempt to give a space at the United Nations between East and West during the Cold War, it took the organization into the limbo of an inability to act, and in the worst cases into the limbo of a lack of respect, which is to say of irrelevance. "Impartiality," in the meaning of "geometrically equidistant," "chemically neutral," and "conveniently inactive," was elevated to a myth by practitioners and governments—well meaning, of course, but perhaps unaware that the term quickly became a tool not for those who wanted to give the United Nations room for maneuver, but for those who wanted to paralyze or neutralize its actions.

In other cases, "impartiality" was unnecessary because a choice had already been made by the Charter of the United Nations or by those covenants and normative texts that should have guided the actions of the institution and its "mediators." And there were other cases where indeed it was not the writ of the law, but ethics itself, that should have ruled it out even if requested. Last but not least, many parties to conflicts were too sophisticated to really believe in impartiality or, in some cases, to demand it. This was the reality, very well known to anybody engaged in hard and real negotiations, but perhaps unknown to theoreticians. Unfortunately, the myth persisted to no great advantage for the institution.

Fairness and equal treatment were and are the proactive meanings of "impartiality," but some mistook the word for inability to choose and therefore to make decisions. The fear of choosing was strong and understandable during the Cold War. It was very much the consequence of a non-dialogue, when many were afraid even of words, semantics replaced substance and truth was considered dangerous. It comes from a time and a place where disagreement would necessarily lead to unfairness, which is to say, that to have a different point of view would accordingly lead one to act unjustly and, to be even more germane to our reasoning, from a time and a place where we perceived diversity as a threat. "Impartiality" was projected as an objective and almost scientifically determinable position, one that did not require any selective capacity and therefore no individual choice.

It is perhaps interesting to recall that when the concept began to gain currency, it seemed even to carry with it a connotation of nationality: Scandinavians, and the Swedish in particular, were "impartial." At that time, it was an understandable and practical approach, but it was nevertheless based on the belief that difference of opinion leads to unfairness, and that those who do not share the opinion of either of the two sides in a dispute would, therefore, be "impartial." The emphasis was on the ability not to express any comment in favor of one side or the other, rather than on dedication to the principles on which fairness and justice are anchored. To be even more blunt, and also more truthful, "impartiality" in the United Nations context for too long meant simply not to receive the veto of one or the other of the two major powers: hardly a synonym for fairness. Yet this concept developed, understandably, during times when it was difficult to define facts as they were, for words were dangerous and semantics was queen. For those who doubt the reality of this argument, suffice it to say that the first Secretaries-General and major mediators were sought out, more often than not, in the Northern countries.

The only quality that was, is, and will be needed both for the institution and for the individuals involved is not "impartiality," but rather credibility. Credibility carries with it a much more operative sense, a much more practical sense, a much more fruitful and result-oriented action. The very ambiguity of "impartiality," or the various interpretations of the word, would predicate in favor of the term "credibility" instead. We understand, of course, that credibility, both at the individual and at the institutional level, may be too costly for some. And yet it is possibly the most effective way to communicate the real image of the United Nations as a fair institution.

A dialogue in the context of the United Nations may, therefore, mean less ambiguity, more openness, more truthfulness and, accordingly, more credibility. But does institutional credibility exist without individual credibility? Collective decisions taken by institutions are eventually carried out by individuals. Credibility as the ability to deliver on one's own word is surely more useful than any definition of impartiality. In this regard, decisions taken by the institution that would appear to be "impartial" but could not be implemented may have damaged the organization and its credibility. In the context of our reflection, the double standard is significant insofar as it is the consequence of the inability to listen as well as arrogance. The double standard's effect on the organization is mainly the damage to its credibility. Credibility becomes even more relevant in this day and age when the organization has to withstand not only the judgment of its members but also the opinions of large sectors of civil society able to communicate their voices in a wider and wider sphere. If until yesterday the organization was correctly concerned about the opinion of its members, it would appear that in the future, it has to be equally concerned about the judgment that may be passed on it by different sectors of the population in different countries.

There is no question that the United Nations of recent years, and in particular the Secretary-General, has been cultivating different constituencies above and beyond the member states. Those constituencies may not have the power to vote, and surely do not have military power to exercise in different corners of the world, but they are increasingly able to influence the shaping of this new world. The question really is: what is the new relationship, if any, that can be established between the organization and this new form of nonstructured voices? Here, more specifically, it is a dialogue approach that may be the most appropriate. In fact, it may be the only one available either to the organization or to nongovernmental actors that may make up the new constituency of the organization. They will surely be less sensitive to the finesse of diplomacy and to the subtle language of "impartiality"; they will demand credibility in exchange for their advocacy of human solidarity, which is the only requirement the organization may legitimately ask of them.

The war crimes tribunals of recent years represent a qualitative step forward in the evolution of international society. We recognize that they were nevertheless the result of the political will of some, responsive to the political needs of the times. Their workings may also be the result of political compromises of dubious ethics. All this, however, cannot detract from the fact that like the United Nations itself, they are seriously rooted in political reality while they also contain the potential and the yearning for a higher level of justice and fairness at the international level. There were many who, upon their creation, speculated that this new institution would hamper the possible achievement of peace agreements, because it would seem to come out in favor of justice even at the cost of "peace." Others were quick to criticize the ineffectiveness of those newly born institutions, for they were not proceeding as swiftly as theory would have liked. Time has proven both wrong. More and more indicted people have been brought to justice before these tribunals; in fact, the pace seems to be quickening. Most importantly, the voices raised in favor of compromise at all costs, even at the cost of justice, are less and less loud.

In fact, the tribunals were generated by a mindset that has the courage to make decisions and believe that the hope for justice, if not justice itself, is an indispensable component of what we call peace. We are aware that these tribunals are not perfect in an idealistic sense. They will still be politically subservient to the Security Council in some cases, but they have nevertheless already served the purpose of catching the collective imagination and the aspirations of many across borders. We believe that to read these developments in a positive and, some would say, an idealistic way is the right way to read them because it generates hope. It proves that we can go where previous generations have not gone; and further still, it demonstrates that the United Nations institution is adaptable and flexible enough to catch the wind of new times, to run ahead of the pack and not behind.

From 1945 to 1960, the word that carried the collective imagination of the United Nations was "neutrality." In the years that followed, indeed for the decades that followed, it was replaced by "impartiality." Perhaps the time has come to move further, and have the courage to replace it with "credibility." If "neutrality" projected the image of respect for different opinions without action, and "impartiality" that of equal treatment within the boundaries of the veto, is not "credibility" a better term to project the image of fairness with accountability? The organization, its members, its advocates and its practitioners may well have to have the courage to aim even higher and to use the word "fairness" above all, no matter what the cost.

## Reconciliation

Reconciliation is the highest form of dialogue. It includes the capacity to listen, the capacity not only to convince but also to be convinced and most of all, the capacity to extend forgiveness. In essence, it is dialogue as a basis for the future, not dialogue as a recrimination for the past. To reach this level of dialogue, the perception of diversity as an asset, the re-assessment of the enemy and the feeling of personal responsibility and of belonging may well have to be acquired. The good news is that though it seems impossible at the level of global relations, reconciliation has already happened, not only in many individual cases but also on the larger level of communities. It is therefore possible, not just because it is a vision that can be outlined but also because it is already a reality in some corners of the world.

Accountability after repressive rule or civil war is a way to strive for justice: not a vindictive justice, but a reconstructive justice; not one that forces us to live in the past, but one that frees us from that kind of past and assures its nonrepetition. Reconciliation is a necessary step towards a better society and better individuals. Indeed, it is a qualitative step forward on the long journey of growth of our species. We have already seen that reconciliation, or "transitional justice," as it is being referred to, has taken different forms in different parts of the world. The Truth and Reconciliation Commission in South Africa is probably the most successful to date. In other cases, tribunals of different kinds have been established with some mixed results. In still other cases, nothing has been done, and yet societies have resumed living together without apparent resort to private justice or settlement of accounts. Despite no structural changes, the case of Lebanon can be seen as one of these latter forms for the time being.

The challenge of reconciliation is that it cannot be dealt with exclusively at the institutional level. While institutions and organizations and various instruments will have to be set up for it to occur, much more is required for a true reconciliation to come about. It is not only a challenge for institutions, it is also a challenge for peoples and individuals. In this respect, the answers to questions of how society can respond to past political violence and prevent it from happening again, how perpetrators can be held accountable for their crimes and what obligations are due to victims of past violence have to satisfy, to a great extent, the hearts and the minds of individuals. For only when this happens will patterns of behavior be changed and, most of all, will lives no longer be lived in the past but in the present. Transitional justice, therefore, requires an overall societal approach. In this sense, the separation between peoples and institutions, between individuals and leaders, becomes very tenuous, for everybody has to become involved at more than just a superficial level.

It is a colossal undertaking for any society; it is even more so if one were to decide to take it on at the global level; and it is perhaps an even more difficult task that may go beyond the capacity of traditional institutions. The challenge of reconciliation after repressive rule or civil war may not be achieved by invoking only the rationality that is an integral part of traditional institutions. It may go beyond the "emotionless" efficiency of the rules and laws we have, very appropriately, created. It may need to appeal, therefore, not only to the mind but also to the heart and soul of those who may offer reconciliation and those who may beg for it. Do our institutions have the capacity to appeal to the heart and soul of those who have to take the first step towards reconciliation?

For two hundred years, our institutional setup has been focused on an attempt to detach it from the irrationality of human emotions and the unpredictability of human whims. The reason behind it was understandable, justifiable and correct. However, two centuries after the creation of those same institutions and the attempt to create a legal system based on equality, where nobody would be above the law, where emotions would have no place but mind would be king, we are confronted with the need to appeal not only to the minds but also to the hearts and souls of individuals. Those hearts and those souls have been far removed from the institutions and have been kept at bay as if they would pollute the rationality of the institutional setup. When searching for justice, when aiming at reconciliation, we may well discover that we need to go beyond the mind. Are our institutions equipped for that?

Transitional justice and reconciliation are not only achieved through the rationality of international law and the logic of the almost-mathematical methods of collective decision-making that our institutions have tried to set up. In fact, it may be worthwhile asking the question whether reconciliation can be the son or daughter of the mythical "blind Justice"? For reconciliation is a step beyond justice. It demands a degree of forgiveness that very likely only the best among us will ever be able to reach. Reconciliation in its ultimate form is a faraway objective and ideal and aspiration that could only be achieved globally if each of us individually were to reach a higher state, that of going beyond justice and the hope for it, beyond justice into forgiveness. It is a tall order; many of us may not have the courage or the strength even to move in that direction. After all, how many societies still pursue vengeance in the illusion that it represents strength or honor; how many individuals still feel the need to pass on to their children the hatred they harbor? The unfortunate answer is too many. No wonder, therefore, that institutions may not be structurally equipped for—and, even more, may not be interested in—pursuing reconciliation, for that may appear to be simply an impossible dream. Yet instinctively, we all know that reconciliation is the right path to take. Denial of this may lead us unconsciously in the opposite direction—a perpetual state of hatred, if not a perpetual state of war.

One with firsthand knowledge of the difficulties of reaching reconciliation is Alex Boraine, an architect of the South African Truth and Reconciliation Commission. He notes:

> In decisions on transitional justice, moral and legal considerations are overshadowed by socio-political factors. In fact, the greater the commitment to ending violence and the more that peaceful coexistence is a declared goal of the transition, the greater the political restrictions faced by the transitional government.
>
> The easiest response to the uneasy and uncomfortable demand facing South Africa's new dispensation

*would have been amnesia in the form of blanket am-*
*nesty. To the eternal credit of all involved, this did not*
*happen, and a process was devised which on the one*
*hand met the political demands of the time but on the*
*other introduced a process which made acknowledg-*
*ment and accountability possible. Also, this process kept*
*the spotlight more on the victims and survivors than*
*on the perpetrators. The challenge faced by the new*
*government, in the words of the Interim Constitution*
*of 1993, was to build 'a . . . bridge between the past of*
*a deeply divided society characterized by strife, con-*
*flict, untold suffering and injustice and a future*
*founded on the recognition of human rights, democ-*
*racy and peaceful coexistence.' This bridge was unity*
*and reconciliation: unity over division, reconciliation*
*over retribution, truth over lies and cover-ups, justice*
*over impunity. And the hope was that the bridge of*
*unity and reconciliation would lead towards the con-*
*solidation of democracy and a culture of human rights.*

— *Alex Boraine,* A Country Unmasked, *2000*

The reality of equality in vulnerability has shattered a number of myths of our modern era: first and foremost, the myth of invincibility of anyone at all; second, the myth of splendid isolationism; third, the myth of superiority of one race over another; fourth, the myth of knowledge control; and fifth, the myth that we are always right and the others are always wrong. Accordingly, where these myths are crumbling, the Golden Rule is making more headway in public life as well as in private life in a more effective and credible way. With shifting alignments based on issues we may find ourselves at different times to be a vulnerable "minority," an easy victim of discrimination, aggression or injustice. The fear of being unjustly treated is what may have triggered the renewed sense of human solidarity. Human solidarity is cutting across borders. The ease of communication can strengthen human solidarity across the divide, irrespective of existing divides.

Reconciliation is hardly a process that can be imposed or forced upon anyone from top to bottom, and it is a process that becomes successful only when it is carried out at the grassroots level. It has worked better, though, where the hearts and souls of individuals have been called into play by the voice of courageous leaders. Far from being necessarily the result only of a "mass movement," reconciliation seems to require the charisma of principled leaders in society who would take the risk, in some cases to sacrifice their lives for their beliefs. The assassinations of leaders who have tried to cross the divide, who have gone beyond hatred, have been and will continue to be not just the assassination of one person, but also the destruction of hope for so many and for so many years. We have witnessed cases in the last ten years where this has happened, and we have seen how the assassination of such leaders has taken history backward, in some cases so far backward that we cannot see how it will change direction yet again. Reconciliation, and the refusal to believe that vengeance is justice, may well be the cutting edge of a social ethics that is yet to come in the larger scale. The great encouragement that we can draw from South Africa, Southeast Asia, Europe and South America in different ways and in different degrees over the last ten years is that we have seen shining examples of leaders who have gone the way of reconciliation, in some cases with great success, in some others just to encounter their own death.

What is sad, as we reflect on our recent world history, is the silence that sometimes has surrounded those who wanted to go, and did go, beyond the ethics of violence against violence, killing against killing, blood against blood. Reconciliation, like a star that rises in darkness, has opened new vistas for humankind just as those who have led their people in the opposite direction have set us all back thousands of years in our societal growth. They are still with us, they are still taking us backward and they occupy different positions in society, from humble soldiers to leaders of governments. They are unable to understand that the greatest courage is not to kill the one who stands across the divide, but to look for another way, one that perhaps we have never tried before, one that we have not yet discovered. The so-called "courage" of "might" clearly may hide a weakness of mind. Reconciliation shows real courage and may yet be only for the few; but there is little doubt that those few will be the new leaders, the new vanguard, the new elites, the new heroes in the book of a new global ethic.

Reconciliation seems to include two aspects: it has to respond to the hope for justice, and yet it has to go beyond justice. Both of these aspects require reason, spirituality and the strength to be the first to change direction. Reconciliation, in other words, is the sign of a new beginning, and cannot therefore be pursued by those who look only down at the ground, or are only able to repeat what others say. It can only be pursued by those who are prepared to be the first in changing direction and gazing straight into the future.

Reconciliation is a rejection of the way things were; it is a rejection of the failure of others; it is a rejection of the hatred of others. It is a cry that says, "We will not be contaminated by any of that." It requires confronting the truth. Many practitioners of international affairs may think that confronting the truth and not being afraid of it may be beyond the ability of many so-called leaders, and yet many have begun to do just that. The challenge of truth beyond words has been the first ingredient in the successful cases of reconciliation we have been privileged to witness over the last few years. Reconciliation requires us to confront the need for justice beyond law and beyond institutions— the justice of the soul, the justice of the heart, the justice we all know must exist somewhere, in some dimension or time. Reconciliation demands that we look into the eyes of peace, internal peace, peace with ourselves, first. We will not make peace with our neighbor if we are unable to make peace with ourselves, individually and profoundly, honestly. Reconciliation will demand the inexplicable and yet instinctive acceptance of belonging, of partnerships with our fellow human beings—a partnership and a fellowship that is proven by the cases of human solidarity that move a parent to save the life of a child in danger, irrespective of whether that child is of his or her enemy.

Reconciliation may be just beyond the reach of petty politicians, minor figures in the long path of history who will be lucky to be forgotten but more truthfully should be remembered for the damage they did to human societies. Reconciliation is not for the weak of heart, but rather for those who know that they may yet discover how to achieve it and are prepared to search for it. In every given case, in every society, the ways to go about it are bound to be different. It is reconciliation that may lead all of us, no matter how this reconciliation process is achieved, to discover and to establish a global ethic. A global ethic for institutions and civil society, for leaders and for followers, requires **a longing and striving for peace, longing and striving for justice, longing and striving for partnerships, longing and striving for truth.** These might be **the four pillars of a system of a global ethic** that reconciliation, as the new answer to the vicious circle of endless hatred, is going to provide us. Can reconciliation open the door and provide an answer to the dilemma of whether human nature is unchangeable or can be improved? Reconciliation is more than just a political process to answer the questions we have asked at the beginning of these pages. It is more than just an answer to the question of providing accountability after repressive rule or civil war.

> *The crucial task is to fundamentally strengthen a system of universally shared moral standards that will make it impossible, on a truly global scale, for the various rules to be time and again circumvented with still more ingenuity than had gone into their invention. Such standards will truly guarantee the weight of the rules and will generate natural respect for them in the societal climate. Actions proven to jeopardize the future of the human race should not only be punishable*

*but, first and foremost, should be generally regarded as a disgrace. This will hardly ever happen unless we all find, inside ourselves, the courage to substantially change and to newly form an order of values that, with all our diversity, we can jointly embrace and jointly respect; and, unless we again relate these values to something that lies beyond the horizon of our immediate personal or group interest.*

— *Václav Havel, President of the Czech Republic, Prague, 2000*

*What is clear is that for the first time ever the pursuit of a goal by humanity, the attempt to move in the direction of a minimal consensus of shared values, attitudes and moral standards, will require the same degree of commitment and equal contribution of women and men.*

— *Mary Robinson, United Nations High Commissioner for Human Rights*

*By providing a starting point that all can agree upon, a global ethic would begin to traverse the split between subject and object. It would identify the fundamentals that are common to all religious traditions, and distill from them the essence of human belief. A global ethic should constitute a core of belief, acceptable to all. It should not seek to impose one vision, or to legislate away our differences. It should strive for unity, but seek neither to eradicate nor to compromise diversity. After all, in this global age, only a truly global ethic can be of real value.*

— *HRH Prince El Hassan Bin Talal of Jordan*

*The challenge we now face is for the different nations and peoples of the world to agree on a basic set of human values, which will serve as a unifying force in the development of a genuine global community.*

— *Aung San Suu Kyi of Burma, Nobel Peace Prize Laureate*


*Globalization, a priori, is neither good nor bad. It will be what people make of it. No system is an end in itself, and it is necessary to insist that globalization, like any other system, must be at the service of the human person; it must serve solidarity and the common good. . . .*

*As humanity embarks upon the process of globalization, it can no longer do without a common code of ethics. This does not mean a single dominant socio-economic system or culture which would impose its values and its criteria on ethical reasoning. It is within man as such, within universal humanity sprung from the Creator's hand, that the norms of social life are to be sought. Such a search is indispensable if globalization is not to be just another name for the absolute relativization of values and the homogenization of lifestyles and cultures. In all the variety of cultural forms, universal human values exist and they must be brought out and emphasized as the guiding force of all development and progress.*

— *Pope John Paul II, address to the Pontifical Academy of Social Sciences, Rome 2001*


*We are committed to the development of a basic common ethics that may lead societies from mere existence to meaningful co-existence, from confrontation to rec-*

*onciliation, from degeneration of moral values to the restoration of the quality of life that restores the presence of transcendence in human life. Global culture must be sustained by a global ethics that will guide the relations of nations with each other and with the creation, and will help them to work together for genuine world community. Such a global ethics, the idea of which was launched by the Parliament of World Religions in 1993, should not reflect the Western Christian ethos; it must be based on a diversity of experiences and convictions. The church, together with other living faiths, should seek a global ethics based on shared ethical values that transcend religious beliefs and narrow definitions of national interests. Human rights must be undergirded by ethical principles. Therefore, dialogue among religions and cultures is crucial as the basis for greater solidarity for justice and peace, human rights and dignity.*

*— Aram I, Catholicos of Cilicia, Official Report to the 8th Assembly of the World Council of Churches, Harare, Zimbabwe, 1998*

The "seven social sins of human kind," which can be overcome on the basis of a global ethic, are:

*Politics without principles,*
*wealth without work,*
*enjoyment without conscience,*
*knowledge without character,*
*business without morality,*
*science without humanity,*
*religion without sacrifice.*

*— Mahatma Gandhi*

Does reconciliation embody a new global ethic?

At the more operational level, is there a role in reconciliation for international organizations? If reconciliation is the result of a grassroots process, or at least a process that involves the grassroots, if it is a process that involves more than reason, that is, the heart and the soul, is there a role for outsiders, those who are neither the victims nor the culprits? Is there a role for those who can neither offer forgiveness nor beg for it? If conflict resolution is a "legitimate" role for an international institution, is reconciliation a more appropriate role for the new "power structure" of our time and age, namely, for individuals, the nongovernmental groups and the very local institutions?

Reconciliation cannot be taught or imposed. It does not appear to be a technique. It may well defy rationality. Nevertheless, there are two major aspects of reconciliation that should be beneficial to more than just the immediate culprit and victims. On one side, reconciliation embodies the elements of the global ethic; on the other, it defies the very logic of the old paradigm—the paradigm of governance through exclusion, of governance through enemy, of "us and them." Can these benefits be carried through beyond the localisms of where the reconciliation occurs? They appear to be too good to be "lost," and yet the answer is not evident. It may well be that the United Nations will have to become "local" to really be a contributor to a reconciliation process, and furthermore, it may become the international amplifier of the success of local reconciliation into the world scene. Again, neither of these two so-called roles is easily transformed into managerial instructions, let alone into another "restructuring" of the system. We can only begin to envisage a way to do so, but we can hardly claim to have the answer.

Can the United Nations play the role of a witness to the unveiling of the truth? Can it become a guarantor for the commitments that the victims and the culprits are prepared to make as the process of reconciliation moves forward? Can the United Nations become a depository of the process and the uniqueness of each case? Can the United Nations be the listening device and the amplifier for those who wish to obtain inspiration and encouragement from one individual case of reconciliation and perhaps move on to devise a matching reconciliation process within their own local domain? Can the United Nations become the place where we confront the truth, the shame and the abyss of ethnic cleansing, for the United Nations was present when that happened? At the same time, can the United Nations become the place where we rejoice for the victory of the human spirit, which has been able to go through the pain with the dignity of forgiveness to reach reconciliation?

Is the Dialogue in its simplicity, and yet in the dimensions we have tried to present in this short book, an instrument that the United Nations can use to nurture the seed, to engender a process of reconciliation that can only be carried out by the involved parties but perhaps can be encouraged by outsiders? If dialogue is a frame of mind that allows us to listen and to hear, and to be persuaded as much as to persuade, then it can become an instrument for the United Nations to ignite the **hope for**

**reconciliation.** Can the United Nations contribute by shining the light of the truth into the darkness of the abyss and illuminating the road into the future, one of healing and forgiveness? Perhaps reconciliation, in the context of the United Nations, is the telling of the human story without masks, coming to terms with the past in order for the future to be different.

Yet the better role for the United Nations in the processes of reconciliation may be as a helping hand in changing the mindset of individuals, more specifically, to change the mindset that perceives diversity as a threat to a mindset that can build on the commonality of our human condition. More specifically, the commonality that so strongly unites us, even though it is rarely uttered, is our desire to offer a better, a more just, a more peaceful life to our children. As much as changing the mindset of others may appear to be idealistic to some and illusory to others, we have all been witnesses in our local or national realities to the power of those who had such a different mentality. A mindset may well be influenced by books, sermons or even words, but nothing is more persuasive than deeds. Heroes have risen in human history because they lived their principles.

The reports issued by the United Nations Secretary-General investigating what went wrong in Rwanda and in Srebrenica have been an incredible example of facing the truth from an institutional point of view. The courage in undertaking those investigations, the transparency of the results, the accountability that was thus demonstrated and the willingness to face the truth are a great example of how an institution can evolve and acquire more credibility, even when it has to admit mistakes. Some may say that the investigations into Rwanda and Srebenica were the results of the world's demands for accountability and transparency. This indeed is the point: the world at large required such accountability and transparency, and the organization that represents that world public opinion responded accordingly.

There are those who may confuse reconciliation with appeasement, and others who will confuse justice with retribution. As we are writing these lines after September 11, 2001, much of this seems to be relevant. Many could say that we are anticlimactic, for the accusation of appeasement and retribution, whether uttered or not, seems to be in the minds of many. We, however, believe the tragic terrorist attacks of September 11 make the call for a Dialogue among Civilizations even more compelling. Perhaps those who belittled this concept in previous times, those who dismissed it as an academic exercise and those who thought it was a luxury in societies with more immediate needs may perhaps think again. Looking at those who were murdered because their fault was to be "different" from their murderers, and looking at the sense of pervasive vulnerability of minor and major powers alike, of rich and poor, of North and South, then perhaps the call for a Dialogue among Civilizations will appear more concrete, more urgent and, indeed, indispensable. Those who will heed the call for a real Dialogue among Civilizations, both at home and abroad, will send a powerful signal: diversity is not a threat, it is a wealth the world society has yet to fully discover.

*When in despair I remember that all through history
the way of truth and love has always won; there have
been tyrants and murderers, and for a time they can
seem invincible, but in the end they always fall.*

— *Mahatma Gandhi*

The last several years have provided more than one example of innocent civilians' serving as targets of choice in conflicts. Even in the year that the United Nations designated as the Year of Dialogue among Civilizations, major events have occurred that may indicate to some that we are going in the opposite direction. Many may even have given up hope that we can do anything about the apparently unavoidable need for an "enemy."

The fact remains that there are far fewer people in the world who desperately need to invent an "enemy" at any cost, even to the extent of taking innocent lives, than there are people who wish to live in harmony and respect each other's dignity. The terrorists, the irresponsible politicians, the bigots may well be active and vociferous, but they are a minority. They can be noticed because their strong suit is to destroy, and that takes little time and even less courage. To build, to discover, to strive for achievements that will benefit more and more human beings takes more courage and more time. Over our common human history, much more has been constructed than destroyed. In fact, we may well have begun writing a book of global history rather than one about history's end. The demands for peace and justice are not confined to a local reality, and in different ways more and more people believe that neither one nor the other can be achieved locally if they are not achieved globally. The perception, whether right or wrong, of injustice and war is also borderless, as are the efforts to overcome them.

Whether we are moving towards a clash of civilizations, or towards greater human solidarity against those who murder innocents only because they are different, is really up to each of us. The choice is neither predetermined nor unavoidable; that is why each of us individually chooses and takes personal responsibility. We can let the small minority take over and throw us into continuous conflict at all levels; or we can enlarge the coalition of those who respect each other's dignity and common humanity, who value the life of our family members as well as the life of our fellow human beings on the other side of the planet. We are the majority; we come from all corners of the world; we are the builders; all can see our work where peace prevails. We believe in the greatness of the human spirit because we offer positive values and need no enemy to sustain our beliefs.

Our children can do better than we. They can go where we have not gone, they can achieve what we have failed to do, and they can discover what we do not even know exists. They can give new forms to human solidarity and enlarge the common denominator of human values. Many will cross the divide—over and over again, until there will be many more bridges and no more walls.

> *Out beyond ideas of wrongdoing and rightdoing,*
> *there is a field. I'll meet you there.*
>
> — *Rumi*

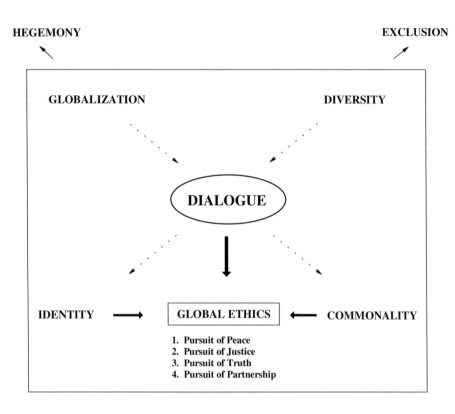

HEGEMONY                                                       EXCLUSION

GLOBALIZATION                             DIVERSITY

**DIALOGUE**

IDENTITY  ⟶  GLOBAL ETHICS  ⟵  COMMONALITY

1. Pursuit of Peace
2. Pursuit of Justice
3. Pursuit of Truth
4. Pursuit of Partnership

Figure 4

*Unsung Heroes*

# Dr. Faouzi Skali, *Morocco*

Disturbed by the grievous state of international relations in the Persian Gulf during the 1991 war, Dr. Faouzi Skali, an anthropologist with a background in mystical Islam, searched for common spiritual and cultural means to reduce the tensions between the Middle East and the West. To reach across the divide, and to begin mending the rift, he envisioned an exchange of sacred music.

The Fez Festival of World Sacred Music, under Dr. Skali's direction, has underscored the connection between people as musicians and as spiritual beings. Every year, the festival brings together artists of different faiths and cultural heritages to facilitate a dialogue through the common ground of music. The festival has demonstrated that musical harmony can draw unlike groups together as few other endeavors can.

In the 1996 Fez Festival, Skali invited an orchestra of supposed rivals of Bosnian, Serbian and Croatian descent to play the sacred music of their Muslim and Christian roots. The ensemble characterized what Dr. Skali had set out to accomplish from the start. Despite having been labeled as enemies in their homeland, the members of the orchestra performed a concert that demonstrated the borderless world of music and song. Through music, Dr. Skali has enabled performers and audiences alike to discover their unity while celebrating the beauty of their diversity.

The spiritual music of the annual festival has the power to engage people beyond physical appearances and cultural or linguistic differences. Through Dr. Skali's vision and leadership, harmonious relationships formed at the Fez Festival have changed the way that people approach "the other."

# Dr. Salahuddin Ramez, *Afghanistan*

A war zone in a faraway land is a place that many would dread, and few would hazard to venture into. Yet there are those who have braved the threat of disease, the terror of violence and the fear of the unknown in order to attend to others. Dr. Salahuddin Ramez was one of those selfless individuals who faced the precariousness of the war zone and highly contagious diseases in order to provide hope to and ease the suffering of people unknown to him.

Since 1995, after leaving the familiarity of his native Afghanistan, Dr. Ramez worked in Pakistan, Sudan and East Timor. As a surgeon for the International Committee of the Red Cross, he went into some dreadful situations, repeatedly risking his own health and security to provide a chance for survival to the sick and wounded.

Tragically, the risks he took in order to serve others in need would eventually contribute to his own demise. During the course of duty in eastern Sierra Leone, he was fatally struck with a tropical illness, Lassa fever. Humanitarian workers like Dr. Ramez are especially vulnerable to the disease, which spreads from person to person through contact with human body fluids.

His is not just a very sad story of someone's dying in the line of his or her routine work. It is a compelling story of an individual who took very seriously his responsibility for the well-being of others. It is a powerful memorial that shows one person's sensitivity and concern for other people, going far beyond his religion or culture.

# Zlata Filipovic, *Bosnia*

In September 1991, Zlata Filipovic began keeping a diary, as many young children do. In the beginning it is filled with the innocent escapades and carefree amusement of a clever, energetic girl from a middle-class family in Sarajevo. Then, less than one year later, her childhood jubilance was visibly shed as her diary entries moved from the typical stories of an eleven-year-old schoolgirl to the dark and depressing reality of a Bosnian war zone.

Her playtime and parties, skiing and piano lessons were soon replaced with time spent sitting quietly in a cold cellar. There she would be safe from shelling and the sniper who lurked in the hills above her home. Under the dim light of a candle, she wrote vividly about her grief for her lost friends, the suffering of her family and her ruined Sarajevo.

With the dramatic changes that took place, her innocence was swept from her as she quickly learned to cope with hunger, thirst, cold and darkness. Priorities changed and Zlata matured quickly. She developed an uncanny immunity to the sound of shelling—not befitting a child—and became easily satisfied with less and less.

Despite the war, she managed to carry on through the support of her parents and the catharsis of her writing. Zlata remained strong for her family and had a gritty determination to survive and to experience even a few pleasures. She learned to face the difficulties of war and stepped up to assume adult duties of fetching water, conserving food and fuel and looking out for the safety of others.

What is most extraordinary is that for her age, she remarkably expressed the futility of war and the divisive nature of politics. Zlata, of a mixed ethnic background, wrote: "Among my girlfriends, among our friends, in our family, there are Serbs, Croats and Muslims. It's a mixed group and I never knew who was a Serb, a Croat or a Muslim. Now politics has started meddling around . . . it wants to separate them." Her diary was first published by UNICEF.

Never losing sight of the injustice of the political cleavage of the Bosnian community into three groups, she now uses her time to foster communication between different cultures. She has been instrumental in the work of UNICEF on Children in Armed Conflict, and is also a consultant to the UNESCO jury for children's literature on tolerance.

Today, Zlata is a symbol of courage for children lost in the mire of war. Even as her pain was the result of the failure of our leaders, her moral concern is a sign of the peace and hope embodied in her generation.

# Jack Beetson, *Australia*

When the land occupied by Australia's indigenous peoples was penetrated more than two hundred years ago, the aboriginal traditions, forms of government and educational system were threatened and in some cases even erased. Today, while the possibility for the blurring of indigenous culture still exists, Jack Beetson affirms that "We (indigenous) are not disappearing . . . while we have our cultures, we will survive."

Beetson, an indigenous educator from Australia, preserves the uniqueness and identity of his people by engaging both indigenous and non-indigenous peoples in the search for inclusive solutions. Year after year, he brings both groups to his remote Linga Longa Philosophy Farm to promote a comfortable dialogue around the campfire on issues of aboriginal identity, culture and reconciliation.

In addition to these workshops, as Executive Director of the Co-operative for Aborigines Limited (Tranby Aboriginal College in inner Sydney Glebe), Beetson arranges for cultural exchange in the classroom. The cooperative welcomes all people regardless of cultural heritage and offers something unique for each group. For the aborigine who has been separated from his or her people and culture as a child, the cooperative renews identity, helps claim the pride of the ancestors and introduces challenges such as reconciliation. The non-aborigines at the cooperative may leave the city classroom and spend weekends in a lush bush environment, learning about the history of the land and, inevitably, their role in preserving aboriginal traditions through respect.

Over the years, Beetson has taught thousands of non-aborigines about the indigenous way of life by sharing an intimate experience with nature and his culture. This experience may cultivate a change in behavior and an appreciation of the "other" that could not have been achieved at a distance.

For his own people, Beetson has been instrumental in advocating self-determination in education for aborigines, and he continues to strive for justice and rights worldwide for aborigines. A local mentor and international hero, Beetson has gently paved the way for reconciliation and a new mode of intercultural relations.

Given the struggles faced by his people and ongoing injustices faced by indigenous peoples worldwide, Jack Beetson could have resigned himself to frustration and indignation. Yet as a courageous and visionary individual, Beetson placed his confidence in dialogue and the belief that reconciliation can be achieved for all people who now share the land that his ancestors nurtured for fifty thousand years.

## Margaret Gibney, *Northern Ireland*

At age twelve, Margaret Gibney became part of the legacy of individuals who inspire entire nations and move world leaders to action. Margaret along with other students in her class wrote to world leaders asking for messages of hope and peace for the "Wall of Peace Project." Growing up in Northern Ireland and knowing little else but war, she wrote to British Prime Minister Tony Blair. The response was overwhelming.

The prime minister was touched by the concern of a child who was living a childhood rife with violence. What struck him as he read her letter on American television and in the House of Commons was the grim reality that Margaret, as stated in her letter, had "only known one year of peace in her whole life."

Her words were at once echoed throughout the United Kingdom and the United States, initially by Prime Minister Blair, and then by a flurry of media who sought out the previously unknown girl. By simply expressing her hopes as a child, as a student and as a member of her community, she became a powerful voice of peace. As a result of her letter, she met and introduced President Bill Clinton at a peace conference in Northern Ireland.

Margaret became a Young Ambassador for UNICEF and a spokesperson for children who, like her, had their childhood stolen by war. For both her local and her international efforts, she has been officially recognized as an advocate for peace.

Her honest and sensible plea to the prime minister carried with it an indomitable message. It was a simple gesture, yet it may have been more profound than anything that leaders on either side have been able to impart for decades. Without intending to draw attention to herself, she inadvertently became a role model for her peers and a symbol of hope for her troubled Northern Ireland.

Margaret's resolve that better things will come is evident in her poem *The White Dove:*

> *Think of how lovely*
> *Peace could be,*
> *The people of Belfast*
> *Fearless and free.*
> *As time goes by,*
> *We'll learn to love*
> *The sign of peace,*
> *A pure white dove.*

# Sydney Possuelo, *Brazil*

As a child, Sydney Possuelo heard stories of two young brothers, Orlando and Claudio Villas Boas, who worked earnestly to find and protect each endangered tribe in the Brazilian Amazon. Sydney knew this was the way that he, too, would spend his life.

As the head of Brazil's Department of Isolated Indians, a branch of the National Indian Foundation, Sydney scours the jungle for months on end to confirm the presence of a tribe. By tracking tribes previously unknown outside the rainforest, he is striving to protect the people and their original way of life from the encroaching threats (illness, builders, loggers and material goods) that accompany modernity. Once a tribe is identified, he then navigates his way through the appropriate bureaucratic institutions responsible for ensuring that the demarcation and integrity of the tribe's ancestral territory are preserved.

There are serious risks involved in pursuing threatened tribes, among them the possibility of attack from those one is seeking to protect, who, understandably, may not distinguish one invader from another. On one occasion, Sydney was ambushed and nearly killed by a fearful Indian's drawn bow, and other persons from his foundation have been killed by tribes defending their territory and community.

While meeting and negotiating with the tribes is a delicate and courageous task, Sydney's program is not universally accepted within the government and the larger society. At times, hostile ranchers, construction companies or others have tried to derail Sydney's efforts to protect indigenous land.

Despite the tremendous risk involved, and the countless hours required to search for the unknown, Sydney remains steadfast in his dream to preserve the human diversity within the Amazon's lush, once impenetrable, domain.

# Dr. Sultan Somjee, *Kenya*

Kenyan ethnographer Dr. Sultan Somjee explores various African peace traditions and transmits those lessons to the wider community through several means. As the founder of the African Peace Museum Project, Dr. Somjee has facilitated the viewing of traditional peace artifacts through Community Peace Museums. He also heads the ethnography department of the National Museum of Kenya in Nairobi.

Dr. Somjee explores the history and the deeper meaning of traditional visual objects and arranges for their display, noting that "these non-reading cultures do not build monuments and they do not write, but they keep alive their knowledge with oral and visual traditions." He explains that traditions such as peace trees are visual symbols unique to the land and cultural artifacts that hold a special meaning of peace. The Peace Trees of the Maasai, according to Dr.

Somjee, "are symbolic of negotiations and a reminder of peace heritage." Accordingly, he has created an outdoor museum of peace trees.

Dr. Somjee works with many communities to preserve the traditional approach to conflict resolution, particularly in areas suffering from civil war or economic hardship. He has discovered that neighboring communities cherish similar ways as tokens of peace. Two ethnic groups who have clashed on occasion, the Maasai and the Pokot, have similar methods of reconciliation. Perhaps by learning about their shared peace traditions, a broader appreciation for other aspects of the groups' commonality may emerge. Others beyond the Maasai and the Pokot, indeed beyond Africa, may learn to engage in dialogue using their local and historical methods of settling disputes among tribes.

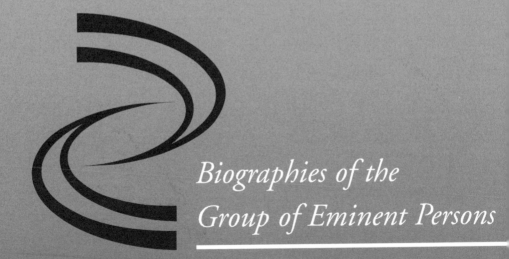

*Biographies of the*
*Group of Eminent Persons*

# Biographies of the Group of Eminent Persons

**Dr. A. Kamal Aboulmagd,** *Egypt*

Dr. Ahmed Kamal Aboulmagd is a practicing attorney in Cairo and a Professor of Public Law at Cairo University since 1958. He earned a Doctorate of Law from Cairo University.

Dr. Aboulmagd served as both the Minister of Youth and the Minister of Information in Egypt in the early 1970s. He has held the distinguished position of Legal and Constitutional Advisor for the Crown Prince and Prime Minister of Kuwait. He is a member of the Supreme Council of Research of the University of El-Azhar in Cairo and a member of the Academy of Magreb. He is also a member of the Egyptian Society of Human Rights and the Egyptian Supreme Council for Women's Affairs and Rights.

Dr. Aboulmagd has published in English and Arabic on constitutional and administrative law, including a pamphlet in Arabic entitled *A Contemporary Islamic Point of View* and a book in Arabic entitled *Dialogue, Not Confrontation,* now in its second edition. For the last twenty years, he has been a judge, vice president and president of the World Bank Administrative Tribunal.

## Dr. Lourdes Arizpe, *Mexico*

Dr. Lourdes Arizpe recently held the position of Assistant Director-General for Culture at UNESCO Paris. She earned an M.A. in Anthropology, followed by a Ph.D. in Social Anthropology, at the London School of Economics and Political Science.

Dr. Arizpe has held several notable international positions. She was the President of the International Union of Anthropological and Ethnological Sciences, and at present serves as Vice-President for the International Social Science Council (ISSC). She also served as Vice-President for the Society for International Development (SID) and as a member of the Steering Committee for Development Alternatives for Women in a New Era (DAWN).

Dr. Arizpe was a member of the World Commission on Culture and Development and Chair of the Scientific Committee of the World Culture Report.

As a research scholar and lecturer, she has received a Fulbright-Hayes and a John D. Guggenheim grant and several awards for her scientific work. She has been a Fellow of the Global Economic Forum of Davos. At present she is a Professor at the National University of Mexico.

Dr. Arizpe has published numerous research articles and chapters of books. Her most recent works include "Culture and Globalization" in *UNDP Working Papers of the Human Development Report* (1999); *The Cultural Dimensions of Global Change: An Anthropological Approach* (Paris: UNESCO, 1996); and "Re-thinking the Population-Environment Debate" in *Population and Environment: Re-thinking the Debate*, Arizpe, Stone and Major (ed.) (1994).


## Dr. Hanan Ashrawi, *Palestine*

Dr. Hanan Ashrawi recently became the Minister of Information for the Arab League. She is an elected member of the Palestinian Legislative Council. She has an M.A. from the American University of Beirut and a Ph.D. in English from the University of Virginia.

Dr. Ashrawi is the founder and Secretary General of the Palestinian Initiative for the Promotion of Global Dialogue and Democracy (MIFTAH). She was the Spokesperson of the Palestinian Delegation to the Middle East Peace Process from 1991 to 1993. She is a Professor at Birzeit University, where she has been Chair of the English Department and Dean of the Faculty of Arts.

Dr. Ashrawi's books include *This Side of Peace: A Personal Account* (1995) and anthologies of poetry, fiction and literary criticism. She serves on the international advisory boards of the Council on Foreign Relations (Washington, DC), UNRISD and other organizations, and is on the Board of Trustees of the Carter Center.


## Dr. Ruth Cardoso, *Brazil*

Dr. Ruth Cardoso is Brazil's First Lady and President of the "Comunidade Solidaria" program, an organization that aims to combat poverty and social exclusion in Brazil through the promotion of partnerships between government and civil society.

Dr. Cardoso received a Ph.D. in Anthropology from the University of São Paulo in 1972. She attended Columbia University as a Fulbright scholar for postdoctoral studies.

Dr. Cardoso is a member of the Board of the United Nations Foundation. She has also served on the editorial board of *Novos Estudos*. She was a member of the Joint Committee on Latin American Studies of the Social Science Research Council and the American Council of Learned Societies.

She has held academic positions at the Graduate Political Science Program, University of São Paulo; the City and Regional Planning Department, University of California, Berkeley; and the Center for Latin American Studies at Cambridge University. In addition, Dr. Cardoso has been both a researcher and director at the Brazilian Center of Analysis and Planning, a member of the Board of the Public Educational TV of the state of São Paulo, a counselor at the National Council of Women's Rights and a member of the Independent Commission on Population and Quality of Life.

Dr. Cardoso is the author of several articles on urban anthropology, social movements and the Third Sector.

## The Honorable Jacques Delors, *France*

Known as the architect of the Single European Act, the first modification of the Treaty of Rome and of the ambitious reform of funding for the European Community, the Honorable Jacques Delors was one of the most influential politicians in the formation of the Europe of the 1990s. He is a graduate in economics, with a diploma from the Center for Higher Banking Studies.

He became President of the European Commission in 1985. During his time at the head of the Commission, there was a major development of its structures, with the reinforcement of European Community financial systems (the White Paper for a single internal market), the signing of the treaty of adhesion with Spain and Portugal and the creation of the Euro as the single European currency.

He was appointed Minister of Economy and Finance in François Mitterrand's first government in 1981. On the local level, he served as the Mayor of Cliché Marcha in 1993.

## Dr. Leslie Gelb, *United States of America*

Dr. Leslie Gelb is currently President of the Council on Foreign Relations. He received his B.A. from Tufts University, followed by an M.A. and Ph.D. from Harvard University.

Dr. Gelb held many notable positions with *The New York Times*, including Editor of the Op-Ed page, national security correspondent and diplomatic correspondent.

When Dr. Gelb was at the U.S. Department of Defense, he earned the Pentagon's highest award, the "Distinguished Service Award."

He is the author of *Anglo-American Relations, 1945–1950: Toward a Theory of Alliances* (1988). He is coauthor of *The Irony of Vietnam: The System Worked* (1980), which won him the American Political Science Association's Woodrow Wilson Award; *Our Own Worst Enemy: The Unmaking of American Foreign Policy* (1984); and *Claiming the Heavens* (1988). In 1985, Dr. Gelb was awarded the Pulitzer Prize for Explanatory Journalism in 1985.


## Nadine Gordimer, *South Africa*

Nadine Gordimer was awarded the Nobel Prize for Literature in 1991. She is a novelist, short story writer and founding member of the Congress of South African Writers.

Ms. Gordimer was an outspoken opponent of apartheid and is active in human rights organizations. She has written numerous books of nonfiction on South African subjects and has made television documentaries, collaborating with her son on the film *Choosing Justice: Allan Boesak*.

Some of her notable books are *The Pick Up* (2001); *July's People* (1981); *None to Accompany Me* (1994); *Writing and Being* (1995); and *The House Gun* (1998).

## His Royal Highness Prince El Hassan bin Talal, *Hashemite Kingdom of Jordan*

His Royal Highness is the youngest son of King Talal bin Abdullah and Queen Zein El Sharaf, and the younger brother of His Late Majesty King Hussein. His family is directly descended from the Prophet Muhammad and is the forty-second generation.

Prince Hassan graduated from Oxford University with a B.A. (Hon.) and M.A. in Oriental Studies. His Royal Highness has also been awarded numerous honorary doctorates from notable institutions worldwide.

Prince Hassan served as His Majesty King Hussein's closest political advisor, confidante and deputy, as well as acted as Regent in the King's absence from the country.

He is the President of the Club of Rome. He initiated, founded and is actively involved in a number of Jordanian and international institutes and committees. In Jordan, he established and now directs the Islamic Scientific Academy; the Tri-annual Conferences on the History and Archeology of Jordan; the Hashemite Aid and Relief Agency; the Center for Educational Development; the Institute for Diplomacy; and, most recently, the new Al al-Bait University in Mafraq.

At the 36th Session of the United Nations in 1981, His Royal Highness proposed the establishment of the New International Humanitarian Order, which led to his being asked by the UN Secretary-General to found and cochair the Independent Commission on International Humanitarian Issues (ICIHI). The final report of the commission was adopted as a resolution at the 42nd General Assembly.


## Professor Sergey Kapitza, *Russia*

Professor Sergey Kapitza is with the Kapitza Institute for Physical Problems (founded by his father, Peter L. Kapitza, a Nobel Laureate in physics) at the Russian Academy of Sciences in Moscow. He is a

Professor of physics at the Moscow Institute of Physics and Technology. At present, he is engaged in global population dynamics studies and is a member of the Club of Rome.

He has been active in the Soviet, Russian and international science circles and is currently Vice President of the Academy of Natural Sciences of Russia and President of the Eurasian Physical Society. Professor Kapitza is also the host of a weekly science and society program for Russian television.

Professor Kapitza's work in applied electrodynamics has led to the development and design of the microtron, a source of electrons, which has become an established accelerator. He has published extensively on matters of science and society.

## Dr. Hayao Kawai, *Japan*

Dr. Hayao Kawai, a scholar of clinical psychology and Professor Emeritus at Kyoto University, is now an advisor to Kyoto Bunkyo University. Until recently, he was the Director General of the International Research Center for Japanese Studies at Kyoto University. He obtained a Ph.D. in Psychology at Kyoto University. He studied at the Carl Gustav Jung Institute in Zürich and became the first Japanese licensed Jungian analyst.

Dr. Kawai served as a committee member of the Central Council for Education and of the Administrative Reform Council, both of the Government of Japan. He was also Chair of the Commission on Japan's Goals in the 21st Century, a private advisory panel set up by the former prime minister of Japan.

His works have been published widely in Japanese and English and have earned him some of Japan's most prestigious prizes in scientific as well as literary fields, including the Asahi Prize (1997) and the Osaragi Jiro Prize (1982) for his book *Fairy Tales and Psyche of Japan*.

Professor Kawai has also been designated as a "Person of Cultural Merits" by the Japanese government.


**Professor Tommy Koh,** *Singapore*

Professor Tommy Koh is currently Ambassador-At-Large at the Ministry of Foreign Affairs, Singapore,and Director of the Institute of Policy Studies. Professor Koh received a First Class Honors degree in Law from the University of Singapore, a Master's degree in Law from Harvard University and a Postgraduate Diploma in Criminology from Cambridge University. In 1984, he was awarded an Honorary Degree of Doctor of Laws from Yale University. He was Dean of the Law Faculty of the National University of Singapore from 1971 to 1974.

He was appointed by the UN Secretary-General as his Special Envoy to lead a mission to the Russian Federation, Latvia, Lithuania and Estonia in 1993. He has been a member of three World Trade Organization dispute resolution panels, two of which he chaired. He was a Visiting Professor at Stanford University in 1995. He was the first Executive Director of the Asia Europe Foundation, from 1997 to 2000.

Ambassador Koh was Singapore's Permanent Representative to the United Nations, New York, from 1968 to 1971 (concurrently accredited as High Commissioner to Canada) and again from 1974 to 1984 (concurrently accredited as High Commissioner to Canada and Ambassador to Mexico). He was Ambassador to the United States of America from 1984 to 1990. He was President of the Third UN Conference on the Law of the Sea from 1980 to 1982. He was Chairman of the Preparatory Committee and the Main Committee of the UN Conference on Environment and Development from 1990 to 1992.

Ambassador Koh is the author of three books: *The U.S. and East Asia: Conflict and Cooperation*; *The Quest for World Order;* and *Asia and Europe.*

**Professor Hans Küng**, *Switzerland*

Dr. Hans Küng is a scholar of theology and philosophy and a prolific writer. He studied philosophy and theology at the Gregorian University (Rome), the Sorbonne and the Institut Catholique de Paris. In addition, Dr. Küng holds numerous awards and honorary degrees from several universities.

Dr. Küng is President of the Foundation for a Global Ethic (Weltethos). From 1960 until his retirement in 1996, he was Professor of Ecumenical Theology and Director of the Institute for Ecumenical Research at the University of Tübingen.

From 1962 to 1965, he served as official theological consultant (Peritus) to the Second Vatican Council appointed by Pope John XXIII.

Dr. Küng is coeditor of several journals and has written many books, which have been translated into different languages, including: *Justification; The Church; On Being a Christian; Does God Exist?; Theology for the Third Millennium; Christianity and the World Religions; Judaism; Christianity; Global Responsibility; A Global Ethics for Global Politics and Economics;* and *Tracing the Way—Spiritual Dimensions of the World Religions.* He was the drafter of "The Declaration Toward a Global Ethic" of the Parliament of the World's Religions in 1993, and of the proposal of the InterAction Council for a Universal Declaration of Human Responsibilities, 1997.

**Graça Machel**, *Mozambique*

Graça Machel is President of the Foundation for Community Development in Mozambique and, since 1999, the fifth Chancellor of the University of Cape Town in South Africa. She has a B.A. in German Philology from the University of Lisbon, Portugal.

Graça Machel was the Minister of Education for the Government of Mozambique from 1983 to 1989.

She is a member of the Board of the United Nations Foundation, the South Centre, UNRISD and other organizations, and has received numerous honorary, humanitarian and academic awards. She was the Special Reporter to the Secretary-General for the Study on the Impact of Armed Conflict on Children.


## Giandomenico Picco, *Italy*

Giandomenico Picco, an Under Secretary General of the United Nations, is the Personal Representative of the Secretary General for the United Nations Year of Dialogue among Civilizations. He is also the CEO of GDP Associates, Inc., in New York City, and President of the nongovernmental Peace Strategies Project in Geneva, Switzerland.

He graduated from the University of Padua with a degree in Political Science. He holds a Master of Arts degree in International Relations and Comparative Politics from the University of California, Santa Barbara, and a diploma in European Integration Studies from the University of Amsterdam.

Mr. Picco served the UN 1973–1992, to the rank of Assistant Secretary-General for Political Affairs. His assignments included the UN operation leading to the release of the Western hostages in Lebanon and the negotiations that brought about the cease-fire between Iran and Iraq. He was also a member of the team that negotiated the Geneva Accords (1998) on Afghanistan. He represented the Secretary-General as arbitrator in the Rainbow Warrior case.

Mr. Picco has received numerous awards and honorary degrees, including the President's Special Award for Exceptional Service from the United States, the Grand Cross of the Order of Merit of the Federal Republic of Germany and the Order of the Cedre du Liban from the President of Lebanon. His personal account of the Lebanon hostage case was published as a book entitled *Man without a Gun.*

## Professor Amartya Sen, *India*

Dr. Amartya Sen was awarded the Nobel Prize for Economics in 1998. He is a Professor of Economics at Trinity College, Cambridge. He was also a Professor of economics and philosophy at Harvard University.

Following a bachelor's degree in Calcutta, Dr. Sen received B.A., M.A. and Ph.D. degrees from Trinity College.

His professional activities include memberships on numerous editorial boards, including *Economics and Philosophy; Ethics; Feminist Economics; Gender and Development; Indian Economic and Social History Review; Indian Journal of Quantitative Economics; Journal of Peasant Studies; Pakistan Development Review; Pakistan Journal of Applied Economics; Philosophy and Public Affairs; Social Choice and Welfare; Common Knowledge; Critic & Review; Theory and Decision;* and *Business and the Contemporary World.*

Dr. Sen publishes widely in publications such as the *New York Review of Books.* His numerous books include *Democracy as Freedom* (2000) and *On Economic Equality* (1997).

## Dr. Song Jian, *China*

Dr. Song Jian is one of the major science and technology policymakers in China. He, serving as Chairman of the Science-Technology Commission of China in the capacity of Vice-Premier (1985–1998), initiated the reform and opening up of science and technology policy across the country. Currently, he is Vice-Chairman of the Chinese People's Political Consultative Conference and President of the Chinese Academy of Engineering. He holds a degree in engineering and a Ph.D. (Candidate of Science) from MBTY, Moscow, and a Doctor of Science degree from the Moscow National Technical University. He is a member of China's Academy of Sciences and a foreign member of the National Academy of Engineering (United States), Russian Academy of Sciences, Swedish Royal Academy of Technical Sciences (IVA), and others.

Over the last four decades, he has made significant contributions to an array of disciplines. Dr. Song led the program design and the launching and positioning of China's first telecommunications satellites. He was responsible for initiating and conducting the country's "Sparks Program," which aimed at alleviating rural poverty and developing rural/township enterprises throughout China. He has also initiated and guided the China's "Torch Program," which spearheaded the development of high-tech industries through the establishment of 53 science parks across the country.

Dr. Song has authored, coauthored or edited eleven books and has written and published approximately one hundred scientific articles. He has received numerous National Awards on Contribution to Science-Technology development and accomplishments in engineering sciences and mathematics. He has also received the Albert Einstein Award (1987), which is the highest recognition by the International Association for Mathematical Modeling for individual science achievements.

## Dick Spring, T.D., *Ireland*

Dick Spring has been a member of Dáil Éireann (Irish Parliament) since 1981. From 1982 to 1997, he was Leader of the Irish Labour Party and served as Deputy Prime Minister in three Coalition Governments—1982–1987; 1993–1994; and 1994–1997. He also held ministerial office in Justice, Energy, Environment and Foreign Affairs.

Dick Spring was educated at Trinity College Dublin and King's Inns, Dublin, and is a lawyer. He is Chairman and Non-executive Director of a number of companies and is International Counsel to the Washington/Boston law firm Mintz, Levin, Cohn, Ferris Glovsky and Popeo.

He was centrally involved in the negotiation of the Anglo-Irish Agreement of 1985 and the Downing Street Declaration of 1993. He cochaired the British-Irish Inter-Governmental Conference in 1993–1997. At their inception, Dick Spring led the Irish delegation to the All-Party Talks in Belfast, which culminated in the Good Friday Agreement. As Foreign Minister, he represented Ireland at the General Council of the European Union, a body he chaired during Ireland's presidency in 1996. He also chaired the European Council of Energy Ministers in 1984. As well as addressing the General Assembly of the UN on a number of occasions, Dick Spring led EU Troikas to the former Yugoslavia, Russian Federation, ASEAN Regional Forum, EU-SADAC, Middle East; and EU Gulf Co-operation Council.

He is a Fellow of the Salzburg Seminar; an Associate Fellow of the Kennedy School of Government, Harvard; and a member of the Council on Foreign Relations Taskforce on Palestine.

### Dr. Tu Weiming, *China*

Dr. Tu Weiming is the Director of the Harvard Yenching Institute. He has been a Professor of Chinese history and philosophy and of Confucian studies in the Department of East Asian Languages and Civilizations at Harvard University since 1981. He earned a B.A. at Tunghai University in Taiwan and both an M.A. and a Ph.D. in History and East Asian Languages at Harvard University. He is the first Professor of Confucian studies at any English-language university, a position awarded to him in 1999.

A member of the Committee on the Study of Religion at Harvard, the Chair of the Academic Sinica's advisory committee on the Institute of Chinese Literature and Philosophy, and a Fellow of the American Academy of Arts and Sciences, Professor Tu Weiming is currently interpreting Confucian ethics as a spiritual resource for the emerging global community. He taught for thirteen years at Princeton University and the University of California at Berkeley on the subject of Chinese intellectual history. Additionally, he taught Confucian humanism at Peking University in Taiwan, the Chinese University in Hong Kong and the University of Paris.

He is the author of major publications in Chinese and English, including *Neo-Confucian Thought in Action: Wang Yang-ming's Youth; Centrality and Commonality: An Essay on Confucian Religiousness; Humanity and Self-Cultivation; Confucian Thought: Selfhood as Creative Transformation;* and *Wang, Learning, and Politics: Essays on the Confucian Intellectual.* He has contributed a section on Confucian spirituality to a forthcoming encyclopedia on the history of the religious quest, as well as an essay for a report of the U.S. President's Committee on the Arts and the Humanities.

### The Honorable Richard von Weizsäcker, *Germany*

The Honorable Richard von Weizsäcker is the former President of the Federal Republic of Germany, serving a rare double term from 1984 to 1994. He was Chairman of the Commission on "Common Security and the Future of the German Armed Forces" until May 2000.

He attended Oxford and Grenoble Universities, followed by Göttingen University, where he studied law and history.

Dr. von Weizsäcker was cochairman of the Independent Working Group on the future of the United Nations (1994–1995). He was one of the "Three Wise Men" who were requested by the President of the European Union, Romano Prodi, to elaborate suggestions for an institutional reform of the European Union in preparation for the integration of new member states (1999). His memoirs have been published as *From Weimar to the Wall: My Life in German Politics* (1999).

# Dr. Javad Zarif, *Iran*

Dr. Javad Zarif has been Deputy Foreign Minister for Legal and International Affairs of the Islamic Republic of Iran since 1992. He is a career diplomat and has served in different senior positions in the Iranian Foreign Ministry and at various international organizations.

Professor Zarif holds a Ph.D. in International Law and Policy from the Graduate School of International Studies, University of Denver. In addition to his diplomatic responsibilities, he is a Visiting Professor of International Law at University of Tehran, where he teaches human rights, international law and multilateral diplomacy.

In the past two decades, Ambassador Zarif has played a leading role in the United Nations, the Non-Aligned Movement and the Organization of the Islamic Conference. He has served as Chairman of numerous international conferences, including the Asian Preparatory Meeting of the World Conference on Racism (2000), the United Nations Disarmament Commission (2000), the Sixth (Legal) Committee of the 47th United Nations General Assembly (1992–1993), the Political Committee of the 12th Non-Aligned Summit in Durban (1998) and the OIC High-Level Committee on Dialogue among Civilizations. He also served as the President of the Asian African Legal Consultative Committee from 1997 to 1998.

Professor Zarif serves on the board of editors of a number of scholarly journals, including the *Iranian Journal of International Affairs* and *Iranian Foreign Policy,* and has written extensively on disarmament, human rights, international law and regional conflicts. His writings include "Impermissibility of the Use or Threat of Use of Nuclear Weapons," *Iranian Journal of International Affairs*, 1996; "The Principles of International Law: Theoretical and Practical Aspects of their Promotion and Implementation," in *International Law as a Language for International Relations* (The Hague: Kluwer Law International, 1996); "Continuity and Change in Iran's Post-Election Foreign Policy," *Foreign Policy Forum*, 1998; and "Islam and Universal Declaration of Human Rights," in *Enriching the Universal Declaration of Human Rights* (Geneva: Office of the United Nations High Commissioner for Human Rights, 1999).

*Index*

# Index

## A

Accountability  82, 86, 128, 129, 144, 147, 148, 162, 166, 167, 197, 201, 205, 212
Arrogance  25, 26, 52, 85, 139, 194
  of ignorance  69, 100, 135
  of power  100

## B

Borderless  22, 101, 102, 106, 134, 163, 214, 219
Borders/boundaries  13, 45, 53, 99, 100, 101, 102, 103, 104, 105, 116, 122, 127, 129, 130, 133, 139, 142, 146, 151, 152, 163, 165, 166, 196, 202

## C

Change, speed and pace of  23, 33, 34, 57
Civil Society  21, 45, 102, 103, 105, 110, 124, 165, 167, 168, 170–171, 172, 177, 186, 187, 194, 205, 231
Civility  16, 77, 78, 86–87, 91
Clash of civilizations  22, 32, 35, 56, 99, 173, 214
Coalition  102, 103, 105, 115, 127, 168, 169, 170, 171, 172, 173, 214, 240
Common Denominator Values  11, 37, 44, 141, 165, 191, 214
Commonality  36, 37, 41, 76, 149, 173, 211, 225, 242
Communication, real-time  22, 102, 103, 135, 147, 171
Credibility  129, 132, 133, 144, 165, 170, 181, 190–196, 197, 212

## D

Decision-making  33, 128, 142, 143, 144, 187
  collective  142, 143, 184, 185, 186, 200
  individual  143
  process  44, 128, 129, 131, 133, 164, 168, 184, 185, 186, 187, 190

# O

"Other" 65, 67, 74, 75, 76, 77, 85, 87, 100, 109, 118, 137, 219, 222
  demonization of the 100, 126

# P

Paradigm
  new 37–41, 40, 101, 103–154, 166
  of exclusion 111, 134, 209
  of inclusion 100, 106
  old 38, 40, 42, 44, 99–102, 107, 111, 123, 126, 128, 134, 143,
    149, 153, 209
  shift 31, 40, 104, 109, 131
Participation 24, 32, 34, 39, 40, 44, 56, 61, 81, 82, 87, 94, 108,
    109, 113, 131, 133, 168, 184–190
Partnerships 125, 204, 205, 231
Peace 53, 63, 67, 73, 76, 84, 85, 87, 105, 111, 112, 172, 181, 188,
    189, 196, 204, 205, 208, 214, 221, 223, 225, 231, 238
Peoples 42, 164, 168, 169, 174, 198
Power
  delegation of 131
  dispersion of 109, 126–134, 162, 175, 187, 188
  new centers of 34, 114, 127, 128, 129, 139, 151, 163, 209
  politics of 188
Primordial ties 23, 59–62
Private sector 165, 177, 183, 184
Public intellectual 166

# R

Rationality 37, 78, 82–85, 91, 119, 199, 200, 209
Reciprocity 66, 74–78
Reconciliation 104, 125, 138, 166, 169, 182, 197–215, 222, 225
Responsibility 12, 38, 39, 41, 71, 72, 78, 86, 88–90, 91, 108, 115,
    136, 139, 140, 142, 143, 146, 148, 166, 184, 220, 237
  collective 38, 41, 143, 144
  individual/personal 35, 38, 39, 104, 108, 109, 141, 142–148,
    151, 166, 197, 214